E.T.S.U. AT TEXARKANA LIBRARY

*Madan Lal Dhingra
and the Revolutionary
Movement*

BY THE SAME AUTHOR

Jallianwala Bagh
New Light on Punjab Disturbances (2 Vols)
Amritsar: Past and Present

Madan Lal Dhingra
(*The Tribune*, Chandigarh)

Madan Lal Dhingra and the Revolutionary Movement

V.N. DATTA

VIKAS PUBLISHING HOUSE PVT LTD
New Delhi Bombay Bangalore Calcutta Kanpur

VIKAS PUBLISHING HOUSE PVT LTD
5 Ansari Road, New Delhi 110002
Savoy Chambers, 5 Wallace Street, Bombay 400001
10 First Main Road, Gandhi Nagar, Bangalore 560009
8/1-B Chowringhee Lane, Calcutta 700016
80 Canning Road, Kanpur 208004

COPYRIGHT © V.N. DATTA, 1978

ISBN 0 7069 0657 8

1V02D3001

Printed at Kay Kay Printers, Kamla Nagar, Delhi 110007

Acknowledgements

In my entire professional career of teaching and writing, my greatest debt is to my teachers: Dr Percival Spear and Sir Herbert Butterfield, who continue to encourage me, and whom I cannot thank adequately, however I may try, but merely record my deepest appreciations for all they have given me these many years so generously.

John E. Frazer read this manuscript and made valuable suggestions for which I am particularly grateful. My thanks are also due to the following members of the Dhingra family for their personal reminiscences and advice: Mrs Shukla Hari Dass, Mukand Lal Dhingra, and Dr H.L. Dhingra. G.R. Sethi, well-known journalist, closely connected with the Dhingra family, allowed me to use the Dhingra family papers, and Dr Sant Ram Seth, ex-MLA, clarified my queries, and I thank them. I record my grateful thanks to Dr S.C. Mittal who shared his research with me as also to Hari Singh and K.L. Tuteja for their help in tracing some material. I am obliged to the authorities of the National Archives of India and the Nehru Memorial Museum and Library for their permission to use their records.

My wife, as usual, has borne with patience and understanding my complete abdication of domestic responsibilities which alone made it possible to complete this work, and I really do not know how to express my gratitude to her.

Preface

It is intended in this work to present a political biography of Madan Lal Dhingra, to analyze how and why Dhingra killed Sir Curzon Wyllie, Aide-de-camp to the Secretary of State for India, Lord Morley, on 1 July 1909 in London, and what impact this event had on contemporary politics; whether this was an individual act on his own initiative, or part of a conspiracy; and if it was a conspiracy, then to explain why the British refused to deal with it as such but preferred to treat it as simply the isolated case of murder.

Historians are inclined to assess and estimate political revolutionaries by their ideology, programme, and activities but tend to neglect what lies within them: the complexity of their motives, the springs of their actions, and the fund of spiritual forces which enable a man to overcome his circumstances. In the case of Dhingra, the basic question has to be answered: How he came to be what he was; how he came to be like that: born in an affluent family that was loyal to the British Raj, temperamentally shy and reserved but turning into a militant revolutionary, and killing his family friend, Wyllie! It is therefore necessary to analyze the whole complex of instincts and passions which lay behind Dhingra's avowed purpose or formulated principle of action; and his entire action has been studied in this work not as an isolated phenomenon, but as an expression of that style of politics which had begun to gain ascendency in the first decade of this century.

We go to history in all humility for seeking answers to those questions which agitate our mind, and in this work, this writer has tried with the help of the past to answer those questions which seemed relevant to him for the understanding of Dhingra, his social background, his urges, his ideology, his action, and the motives underlying it and the age he lived in.

Kurukshetra University　　　　　　　　　　　　　　　V.N. DATTA

Contents

1	The Family	1
2	Young Indian Revolutionaries in London	7
3	The Assassination	32
4	Why Did Dhingra Shoot Wyllie?	44
5	The Impact	59
6	Epilogue	81
	Appendixes	87
	Notes	98
	Bibliography	109
	Index	111

1 The Family

Madan Lal Dhingra belonged to a rich and highly influential family of Amritsar which contrived to keep a handsome establishment, lived in a expensive style, and cultivated the friendship of high British officials. He was born about 1887.[1] His father, Sahib Ditta Mal, had qualified as Sub-Assistant Surgeon from Medical School, Lahore, in 1867. On his retirement as Civil Surgeon at Hissar, he settled down in Amritsar where he owned large property. The Dhingra family had migrated to Amritsar from Sahiwal in District Sargoda (West Punjab) about 1850. Rai Sahib Ditta Mal built half-a-dozen bungalows on the Grand Trunk Road, and twenty-one houses in Katra Sher Singh in Amritsar. He had inherited ten squares of agricultural land in a village known as Sangiwala (or Moza Sahib Ditta Mal in Chak 574 Nankana Sahib) in District Sheikupura (now in Pakistan). He had also a mansion at his ancestoral place Sahiwal which he made over to his son-in-law. After retirement, he was Hon. Physician and Surgeon to Maharaja Pratap Singh of Jammu and Kashmir, and as Eye-Surgeon his private practice in Amritsar brought him great fortune. He made money without stint. According to his will, which is in the possession of G.R. Sethi who was a tenant of the Dhingra family for many years, his assets were worth Rs 5,30,000 which he claimed as self-earned.[2] His sense of self-respect forbade him to be a parasite.

Sahib Ditta Mal was a crusty old man, highly intelligent, versatile, dynamic, taciturn, dour and bit of a faddist. He had seven sons and a daughter: Kundan Lal, the eldest son, widely travelled, was a flourishing businessman in textiles; Dr Mohan Lal, educated in England, author of several books on medicine, was Health Officer at Amritsar; Dr Behari Lal, M.R.C.P. (London), well-known for his book on physiology, was Chief Medical Officer in Jind State; Chaman Lal first practised law as barrister in Amritsar but later the Punjab High Court appointed him as Official Reciever to the Court of Insolvency at Amritsar; he married Keshub Chunder Sen's grand-daughter, niece of the Maharani of Cooch Bihar; and Chuni Lal, another barrister in the family, was Munsif in Jammu. At this time, around 1906, Madan Lal was studying Mechanical Engineering in London; and his younger brother Bhajan Lal had recently joined the bar; Kaki Rani, Sahib Ditta's only daughter, was married to Chetan Dass of Sahiwal, a big landlord who died young. Thus the Dhingra family, highly educated, widely travelled, cosmopolitan in outlook, ambitious and fairly well-connected with the British official hierarchy with a strong flair for professions like medicine, law, and business, enjoyed a social position not only in Amritsar but Punjab.

There is singularly little known about Madan Lal Dhingra's early life.[3] He passed his First Arts Examination in second division from the Municipal College, Amritsar (subsequently abolished) and joined the Government College, Lahore, but only for a few months. His father stopped his formal education at this stage and induced him to take up business. He served for some time in the Kashmir Settlement Department, and was employed later in the Kalka-Simla Tonga service under his distant relation Rai Bahadur Daulat Ram.[4] This sudden termination of his studies deeply perturbed Madan, and he began to drift in the idle habit of brooding over things, and doing nothing. He became gloomy and disgruntled, and his eccentricity, according to his brothers' testimony, seemed to have gone worse during this period.[5] In despair he ran away from home and joined as Lascar in a ship.[6] He found that a seaman's lot was not to his liking, and this proved to be a blind alley. After five or six months "wild life" he returned home. His brothers then tried to persuade their father to send him to England for higher studies in engineering but the old man was adamant. Sahib Ditta had a great fascination for England, and he wanted his sons to be educated in England but in Madan's case he was reluctant because Madan did not inspire his confidence.[7]

Sahib Ditta had always kept his sons at a distance. He was autocratic and somewhat rigid. What he said was law, and no child could speak back to him, but somewhere in him there was a deep kindness that he was careful never to show on the surface. Madan's brothers continued to plead his cause with their father who ultimately yielded to their importunities, and allowed him to proceed to England. The family hoped that the English climate and environ-

The Family

ment might enable Madan to get rid of his eccentricities, and make a new man of him. Madan left for England in May 1906. He was then about twenty-two, of good height, with a solemn pale face, large staring eyes, cultured, sensitive, shy, somewhat obstinate, and a little awkward; the most striking feature of his personality was his strong will, and a one-track mind. But he had grown up with a painful consciousness of whirling from one scene to another with no solid ground to plant his feet.

While in India, Madan did not take part in any political activity. He was rather too young for it and, moreover, his home town, Amritsar, was then hardly the place to give him any opportunity for training in politics. The Amritsar Municipal Committee was the pivot of the activities of both the British and the Indians. The period before 1910 in the town was primarily a period of growth of civic duties reflected in the proceeding of the Municipal Committee when officials and non-officials sat together, reviewed items, argued, and ultimately in a spirit of amity arrived at decisions. There was then no appeal to the public or discussion of these issue in the press.[8] The main interest of the government was that in Municipal Administration "politics" should be kept out; men favourably disposed towards the rising freedom struggle were frowned upon. The men of the town interested themselves mainly in matters of public import such as the Municipal elections, receptions of official dignitaries, charitable schemes, social and religious functions, planting of gardens, and improving sanitary conditions. The Shining Club was founded in Amritsar in 1907 but its object was purely social, to promote a sense of discipline among its members; but it had no political aim. Political activity began only with the arrival of Rash Behari Bose[9] in Amritsar in 1915 when he took over the *ghadr*[10] agitation with the assistance of Sachin Sanyal[11] and the Maharashtrian Vishnu Ganesh Pingley[12] who began making bombs in the city. These developments were to take place much later.

Amritsar was then politically quiescent and to illustrate this it will here suffice to quote the observations concerning it of the provocative and highly-strung Lieutenant-Governor of the Punjab, Sir Michael O'Dwyer, who contended that the people of Amritsar were of loyal disposition. In the course of a speech delivered at a Durbar held in Amritsar on 17 February 1919, he said:

During the past 5 years, I have paid Amritsar many visits, sometimes when the internal situation was serious, to seek your counsel and support, sometimes to appeal to the loyal martial tradition for which Amritsar is famous when men were wanted to defend the Empire, or money to provide the sinews of war, sometimes to discuss with your representatives important schemes for the improvement of your great and prosperous city. Whatever was the occasion, I always found from Amritsar and its people a prompt and practical response, and I have always gone away heartened and stimulated by the spirit of loyal endeavour and practical co-operation which Amritsar has shown. It is to prove my appreciation and Government's recognition of these qualities, that I have come here to-day....[13]

O' Dwyer's successor, Sir Edward Maclagan, characterized Amritsar as "one of the most peaceful cities in India, known for its religious association, its commercial activity, its Municipal development, and its educational institutions";[14] and he was puzzled as how this peaceful and quiet city could become in 1919 a "centre of sedition."

In the early years of this century the majority of the people in Amritsar lived within the city enclosed with a wall built by Maharaja Ranjit Singh; there were, however, a few bungalows in the civil lines, occupied by British civilians, and other Europeans which were shaded by tall trees and connected with metalled roads. Near the Hall Gate (built in 1876, and named after Col. C.H. Hall, the Deputy Commissioner, Amritsar), the locality of Katra Sher Singh was inhabited by Indians belonging to the upper strata of society; flourishing businessmen, lawyers, and doctors. Sahib Ditta owned in this locality a row of spacious houses known as the "Dhingra buildings."

The social leaders of the town were the *Rai Sahibs* and *Khan Bahadurs* who were held in high respect by the populace because of the influence they wielded with the local administration. Naturally the local British officials gave them patronage for administrative reasons, and used them for carrying out their policies. Some of the prominent members of this class who enjoyed special social position were Rattan Chand Mehra, a lucrative trader, Sunder Singh Majithia, a landlord, Sir Todur Mal Bhandari, Bar-at-law, Nand Lal, a philanthrophist, Pandit Sarb Sukh, a physician, Babu Kanhaya Lal, advocate and landlord, Pandit Kotu Mal, a mill

The Family

owner, Sir Gopal Dass Bhandari, a vakil, Sardar Jeewan Singh, a tehsildar, Khawaja Ghulam Sadiq, Bar-at-law, Yusuf Shah, a landlord, Gagar Mal, a landlord, and Rai Sahib Sahib Ditta. These men had wealth, property, and charitable trust to their credit. They were catholic in outlook, temperate in their demands, cautious in their methods, and more mindful of the benefits of reciprocal compromises.[15] They preferred to live in English style; read the *Civil and Military Gazette* for their morning paper (a staunch Imperial institution) and usually spent their evenings in a club with whiffs of cigars and swigs of scotch. They dressed mostly like Europeans, using even suspenders with their trousers and walking with sticks like English countrymen, though the majority of them wore turbans. They admired the glory of British rule and regarded it as a blessing for the regeneration of India.

The Dhingra family had close associations with some of the high British officials. Sahib Ditta had been Civil Surgeon at Hissar in 1896 when Dunlop Smith was Deputy Commissioner there and friendly relations grew between the two. Later Smith became the Private Secretary to the Viceroy, Lord Minto. Sahib Ditta had served as Medical Officer for the British Government for about thirty years. Through their father, both the brothers, Dr Mohan Lal and Dr Behari Lal, cultivated cordial relations with Dunlop Smith. When the Viceroy visited Gwalior, Dunlop Smith introduced Mohan Lal to him; and later wrote to the Viceroy complimenting the Punjab Government for having secured the services of a "qualified and efficient health officer like Dr. Mohan Lal" for gearing up the sanitary administration in Amritsar.[16] Both these brothers were the joint authors of the *Minto Health Pamphlet* (1908) dedicated by permission to the Viceroy.[17] On the Muzzaffurpur bomb outrage, 30 April 1908, killing Mrs and Miss Kennedy, the wife and daughter of a local barrister,[18] Chaman Lal Dhingra, Bar-at-law, reacted violently to it and published a letter in the *Civil and Military Gazette*, 11 May 1908, attacking the surreptitious crime. While expressing his deepest sympathies to the Viceroy on the tragedy, Chaman Lal eulogized the benevolent character of the British rule in the following terms:

> We could never have been so happy under any Oriental Government, no other Government would have extended so much to raise us by conferring upon us the blessings of modern

civilization and culture. We have advanced in every way—materially, mentally and morally—and bare justice demands that we ought to be grateful for what they have done in our interest.

Enjoying peace and security in the British regime, we are in a splendid position to develop our resources and to improve ourselves in intellectual, social and religious matters. Association with England is helpful to us in various ways.

I firmly believe in the necessity and the blessings of British rule and because I see that some of our men are grievously misguided and are retarding the progress of our country. I know that such ideas are likely to be pooh-poohed by some people.[19]

The two examples cited above show the loyal attachment the Dhingra family had for the British Government. Madan's other elder brother, Dr Behari Lal, expressed similar loyal sentiments to the British Government in 1908 when he submitted to Dunlop Smith a "scheme of a good residential school for the sons of well-to-do Indians of all creeds, where character may be developed *pari passu* with intellect and where the students would be made god-fearing and loyal in the crown."[20] Dunlop Smith thought that the scheme, though laudable and "conceived in excellent spirit" intending to curb the spirit of disaffection which was gaining ground in some of the educational centres in Northern India was rather too idealistic.[21] But Madan never had any such loyalist sentiments. He was brought up in an atmosphere where his nearest relations openly flattered and fawned on the British, and showed servility in their behaviour, and probably this cringing and garish exhibition of downright servitude created in him more than anything aversion to the ruling power.

2 Young Indian Revolutionaries in London

Madan arrived in London in July 1906 and joined the University College on 19 October for studies in engineering. His brother Kundan Lal was already in England concerning his business, and he helped Madan to arrange suitable lodgings.[1] Like other Indian students who went to London for higher education, he visited India House, which was seething with political discontent. By and large, Indian students felt lonely and somewhat isolated in England, and the English, temperamentally reticent and reserved, seldom mixed with them. There was little opportunity for Indians to enter into British social life except, of course, in clubs and ballrooms where English girls usually avoided dancing with "coloured people." In the hey-day of the British Empire, it was quite natural for the English by force of circumstances and clamour of individuals to show in their attitude towards Indians their blatant superiority and dogged arrogance; and an Indian student was apt to suffer from such social barriers and psychological tensions. The English climate with its mist, rain, cold, and snow did not suit him, and he longed for the temperate weather and the brilliant sunshine of his country; he often complained of the raw, unpalatable food, particularly beef which he would not ever dare to touch. The majority of the Indians who could not adjust to the new English environment tended to release their tension by associating only with their countrymen and keeping themselves aloof from English social circles; and they celebrated their national festivals, a demonstration of their solidarity and search for identity.

From his record of activities in England it is clear that Madan mixed a great deal with his compatriots,[2] and did not shun their company as was common with some Indians of aristocratic bearing who preferred to develop social relations with the English only. Belonging to a rich family, he had enough means to lead an easy life unencumbered with any financial strain; he could live the style of a dandy, dancing, drinking, and visiting all the quarters freely—and because of his family connections, he could also move in English social circle easily.

For explaining Madan Lal Dhingra's assassination of Sir William Curzon Wyllie, one must look rather to England than to India because it was in England that Madan formed his political beliefs, and planned his action. He fell under the spell of Vinayak Damodar Savarkar, the leader of the revolutionary movement in England. Soon after his arrival, Madan is said to have visited India House where he widened his circle of friends; he resided there for about six months from March or April 1908 and also for a month in early 1909.[3] The India House, London, had become the hubhub of revolutionary activities between 1907-1909, and the story how a handful of Indian revolutionaries, young and spirited, fired with passionate idealism, embarked on launching a revolutionary movement in the heart of Imperial power has not been told. It was the programme and ideology of this enthusiastic band which spurred on Madan and others to action.

Shyamji Krishnavarma who can easily be called the architect of the revolutionary movement in England opened a hostel under the name of "India House" on 1 July 1905 at 65, Cromwell Avenue, Highgate, London, as a residential centre for Indians.[4] A man of strong convictions, he would never give in. He led a tortuous life with many ups and downs. Born in a poor family in 1857 at Mandari in Kathiawar, Krishnavarma was educated at Elphinstone High School, Bombay, where he matriculated in first class; graduated from Balliol College, Oxford, in 1882, the first Indian to earn an M.A. degree from Oxford;[5] and was called to the Bar in 1884. He represented India at the Oriental Conference in Berlin in 1881; and distinguished Orientalists like Max Muller and Sir Monier Williams, the Boden Professor of Sanskrit at Oxford were impressed by his meticulous knowlege of Sanskrit literature.

On return to India, Krishnavarma practised law for some time; held high offices in native states: Dewan in Ratlam, and in Junagarh, and was a member of State Council at Udaipur, 1893-95. His services in Udaipur court ended mainly due to Sir William Curzon Wyllie, President in Udaipur who was "instrumental in turning out Krishnavarma out of the State service at the beginning of 1895"; and who "successfully opposed his return to State Service in September of the same year."[6] Krishnavarma, however, obtained temporary employment in the private service of the Maharana of Udaipur in 1893, but when Lord Elgin visited Udaipur in 1896, Wyllie debarred Krishnavarma to be presented to the Viceroyal durbar.[7] These bitter and humiliating experiences rankled in Krishnavarma's heart; he could never forget them. Next year in 1897 he left for England, and settled there until he shifted his headquarters to Paris in 1907.

Krishnavarma had met Swami Dayanand, and was attracted to the ideology and programme of the Arya Samaj. In England he was deeply influenced by the ideas of Herbert Spencer and Frank Harrisson; and on 4 December 1903, as a token of reverence for his mentor, he instituted the Spencer lectureship of £1000 in Oxford University. He lived in obscurity in England for a few years, but in 1905 founded the Indian Home Rule Society with the firm resolve to work for self-government in India. The idea of founding this society was suggested to him by H. M. Hyndman who had made a special study of India's political problems. He published in January 1905 his first English weekly *The Indian Sociologist*, an organ of freedom and of political, social, and religious reforms in which he adopted Spencer's following words as his motto:

> Every man is free to do what he wants provided he infringes not the equal freedom of any man.
>
> Resistance to aggression is not simply justifiable but imperative. Non-Resistance hurts both altruism and egoism.[8]

In the first issue of *The Indian Sociologist*, Krishnavarma wrote[9] that the main idea in publishing this monthy was to "enlighten the British public with regard to the grievances, demands and aspirations of the people of India" and "to plead the cause of India and its unrepresented millions before the Bar of Public Opinion in Great Britain and Ireland." The journal, he warned, would continue to "remind the British people that they can never succeed in being a nation of freemen and lovers of freedom so long as they continue to send out members of the dominating classes to exercise despotisms in Britain's name upon the various conquered races that constitute Britain's military power." He made it clear that he had no political affiliations with any political party but would, he added, continue to expound and propagate for the benefit of his countrymen the "new and profound ideas" of Herbert Spencer.

It was generally believed that Krishnavarma's departure for England was not unconnected with the Rand murders.[10] Krishnavarma was a severe critic of Lord Curzon's regime in India which had subjected the people of India to great suffering. He condemned the Moderates' policy of "medicancy" but admired the Extremists, particularly Tilak and his ideology. He gloated over Japan's victory over Russia as a symbol of Asian victory over the West. His humiliation at the hands of British officials, his disenchantment with the ruthless British administration of India, and his radical ideas on liberty which he had imbibed from some of the British political thinkers roused his ire against the British whom he was determined to bring to their knees. The Benchers of the Inner Temple debarred him on 30 April 1909 from being called to the bar for his "seditionary activities."

Krishnavarma's major contribution was the foundation of India House which became a centre of revolutionary movement in England, and which attracted some of the most energetic youngmen, who dedicated themselves to the cause of their country's liberation. He was too much of an intellectual to inspire a following; but never did he swerve from propagating with his usual passionate zeal revolutionary ideas and programme for India's fight for freedom, and he became thus a festering sore to the ruling classes of India. On the other hand, his austerity and political idealism captured the attention of M.K. Gandhi.[11] Krishnavarma believed in the use of violence for gaining political ends, and recommended to his countrymen the maxim of political morality that "political assassination is not murder, and the employment of force when it is preservative and defensive is legitimate."[12] This legitimacy was grounded in his firm belief that the so-called "political offenders" were shielded by International Law, and so he urged that people ought to defy the absurd and antiquated political systems which perpetuated false political values.

Because of the rigorous vigilance enforced by the British Criminal Intelligence, Krishnavarma thought it prudent to shift his centre of activity to Paris in order to have a free hand in mobilizing the revolutionary struggle and, to entrust his work to a younger man, Savarkar. David Garnet who was friendly to some of the inmates of India House wrote that Krishnavarma was regarded by the British authorities as leader of the most dangerous seditious movement.[13] In July 1907 a question was asked in the House of Commons whether the government intended to take any action against Krishnavarma because of his dangerous activities, but the answer was in the negative.[14] Krishnavarma had realized that he had aroused the close attention of the government which was bound to fetter his hands shortly, and destroy what he had tried to build up single-handed. But Krishnavarma could theorize, not organize; propagate, not fulfil; expound, not practise, and this gap between profession and practice was going to be filled by Savarkar in India House who was more a man of action than a theoritician.

Vinayak Damodar Savarkar popularly known as Savarkar had arrived in England in 1906.[15] Krishnavarma, after consulting B.G. Tilak and B.C. Pal, had instituted six lectureships for "enabling authors, artists and other qualified Indians to visit Europe, America and other parts of the world beyond the limits of India so as to equip themselves efficiently for the work of spreading among the people of India a knowledge of freedom and national unity."[16] On Tilak's recommendation to Krishnavarma, Savarkar obtained the Shivaji scholarship in April 1906 which enabled him to proceed to England in June 1906 for higher studies. It is not necessary to draw Savarkar's biographical sketch here but to highlight those features of his personality, and such conjunction of the circumstances which influenced the formation of his revolutionary outlook.

Born in a middle class Chitpawan Brahmin family in 1883 in a village Bhajur, near Nasik in Bombay Presidency, Savarkar received his school education in Nasik; he was a voracious reader, and composed poetry in Marathi at the age of ten.[17] The plague ravaged Poona in 1897, and the plague-officer Rand was murdered by the Chapekar brothers, Damodar and Balkrishna, who went to the gallows smiling and singing verses from the *Bhagwad Gita*. This heroic example of sacrifice deeply moved Savarkar who decided to dedicate his life to the cause of India's liberation. It is said that he took an oath before the family at Bhagur that he would follow the Chapekar brothers in his fight for India's freedom. He graduated from the Fergusson College, Poona, in 1905. As a protest against the Partition of Bengal he had organized a big bonfire of foreign cloths, and was fined, and expelled from the college residency. Both he and his eldest brother Ganesh Damodar took an active part in politics. They toured extensively in Maharashtra to revive the activities of the secret revolutionary society "Mitra Mela" (the association founded about 1899 in connection with the Ganpati celebration and Ganesh) and organized the youth by imparting to them physical training. Vinayak gave also a new name "Abhinav Bharat" to the society which was modelled on Mazzini's "Young Italy" and his main object was to make the youth patriotic, disciplined, and fearless. During the Partition of Bengal he mobilized public opinion in support of the Swadeshi movement which brought him closer to Tilak; he was also the sub-editor of the *Vihari* newspaper of Bombay.[18]

Vinayak was a disciple of Tilak and a man Sakharan Khare[19] whom he knew quite intimately; he ridiculed the Moderates' politics.[20] Before he reached England, he had emerged into a militant Hindu nationalist stirred to political activity by the tradition and sympathy of the past, and by the heroic examples of Shivaji, Maharana Pratap, Guru Gobind Singh, and others who by their reckless valour and sacrifices had resisted to the last oppression and injustice. Vinayak was about twenty-three in 1906 when he reached England; he was now made of sterner fibre, transcending personal ambition, and determined to fight for his country's emancipation. Fixed in purpose, eloquent in oratory, and magnetic in bearing, he could draw round him a band of young spirited followers whom he filled with passionate love for their country, and intense hatred for British rule in India.

In July 1906 Savarkar was admitted as a student of law to Gray's Inn, one of the four Inns of Court in England. Both Savarkar and Krishnavarma had much in common. Naturally Savarkar was obliged to Krishnavarma for making it possible for him to come to England. Both Savarkar and Krishnavarma had great admiration for Tilak, and strongly believed in the cult of the bomb. Both were "revivalists" in the sense that they glorified the antiquity of ancient Indian culture, but in his political ideology, Krishnavarma was influenced more by Western thinkers like Herbert Spencer than Indian. On the contrary, Savarkar's sources of inspiration and emulation were mainly Indian: Ram Das, Shivaji and Tilak, though he had begun to admire Mazzini and Garibaldi. Krishnavarma was primarily an intellectual, while Savarkar basically a man of action; but both shared in common the passion for the liberation of their motherland. When Krishnavarma left for Paris in order to have a free hand for organizing revolutionary activities, it was Savarkar who took over the management of India House. He established the "Free Indian Society" identified as a recruiting agency for the "Abhinav Bharat."[21]

Ostensibly, India House was to provide board and lodgings to Indian students at reasonable rates; and quite a number of students went to India House attracted by Indian meals and cheaper accommodation. One of the youngmen who felt drawn to Savarkar was Madan. Both Savarkar and Madan had arrived in England in 1906. Savarkar was twenty-three, and Dhingra about nineteen. While Savarkar was of humble origin and simple habits, Madan was aristocratic, and a bit snobbish; Savarkar had a clear ideology, but not Madan; but both of them had a certain toughness of spirit and a one-track mind.

It would be wrong to think that Krishnavarma after settling in Paris severed his connections with India House; he kept in touch with the affairs there, and emissaries from both sides moved to and fro, and until Savarkar left London in 1910, they continued to maintain intimate contact. Krishnavarma controlled the India House through his confidant, S.R. Rana, who visited London quite often to assess activities there, and communicate information about them back to Paris.[22] Rana had also been given the task of managing the financial side of India House. From 1907 to the middle of 1909, India House became politically astir; and the moving spirit behind activities there was Savarkar who gathered round him raw youngmen and imparted to them his passionate patriotism. These youngmen were drawn together to rise against British power at a given signal. Savarkar was by nature stern, brave, and impetuous, easily stirred to passionate protestation; the model of a desperate and determined patriot, calm, self-possessed, dignified in language and demeanour. By his idealism and sincerity of purpose, he gained tremendous influence with the band of these young revolutionaries who were willing to follow his ideology and programme.

After Krishnavarma's shifting his centre of revolutionary activities to Paris, Savarkar became the unacknowledged leader of India House. Besides Dhingra, his other staunch followers were Gandurang Mahadev Bapat, Birendra Nath Chattopadhyaya, Harnam Singh Arora, V.V.S. Aiyer, and Govind Amin. Bapat, born in a poor family in 1880, graduated from Deccan College, Poona, in 1903, took special interest in Sanskrit literature, and went to Edinburgh in 1904 for Mechanical Engineering,[23] where he delivered violent speeches against the British Government in India for which the authorities cancelled his scholarship. After Bapat gave up his studies in Edinburgh, Krishnavarma welcomed him in India House where he began to work actively for the Abhinav Bharat, in 1906-08. Like Bapat, Chattopadhyaya known as Chatto among Indians in Europe too abandoned his studies. Born in a rich Brahmin family, Chatterjee was called to the Bar, in 1906-07, was twice unsuccessful in the ICS, and joined Savarkar in revolutionary activities for which he was expelled from the Inns of Court in 1906-07.[24] A fiery poet and journalist, his revolutionary zeal was strongly criticized even by his younger sister, Sarojini Chatterjee (Mrs Naidu). Another trusted follower of Savarkar was Harnam Singh, son of a District Judge of Amritsar, Aya Singh, whom Savarkar had met on board the ship when he was coming to England for law;[25] and there were others such as V.V.S. Aiyer, a young and brillian lawyer from Rangoon, a zealous extremist, Gyan Chand Varma, Secretary of Abhinav Bharat Sabha, and W.V. Phadke who was preparing for the ICS.

Any one visiting India House between 1906-09 would have been greatly struck by the intensity of revolutionary activities which was gaining momentum. While the political activity in India had reached its nadir due to internal dissensions, the India House presented altogether a different scene of hectic revolutionary activity and propaganda. It seemed as though the Indian political leaders had lost their initiative, and knew not whither they were going, but in England leadership was in the hands of a band of enthusiastic youngmen. Their ideology and programme were clear-cut. These youngmen, raw, somewhat impulsive, easily excitable, passionate in their convictions, and indignant about the style of British administration kept themselves informed about the political development in India. They began to develop their interest in the comparative study of world politics; for example, they were inspired by the fanatical spirit of Irish nationalism, by the example of Mazzini's sacrifices, and by the ceaseless struggle going on in the world for the preservation of Human Rights and Liberty. It was not often that one could see them use with their usual vehemence cliches and maxims culled from a cursory glance of books on political and constitutional history.

It would be wrong to imagine that these youngmen confined themselves only to the study of Western political ideas and revolutionary movements, and paid scant attention to the political developments in India. On the contrary, they took a lively interest in larger political issues in India such as Curzon's repressive policy, the Partition of Bengal, the Swadeshi movement, the deportation of Lajpat Rai and Ajit Singh, Tilak's sentence to six years imprisonment for producing seditionary literature and Khudi Ram's bomb-throwing and execution in 1908—issues which generated considerable heat and agitation.

It is natural that when Indians go abroad and live in England, their view of Indian politics is different; they look at India differently; and they tend to measure Indian politics with the yardstick of Western values. The free political institutions which they see the English enjoy round them bring to their mind the striking contrast between liberty on one side, and despotism on the other. In view of the different type of political climate which these Indian youth breathed in England, the British rule in India appeared to them all the more reprehensible and inhuman. In the initial stages, Krishnavarma, Savarkar, and Bapat organized the whole programme of the revolutionary activity in India House, and created the climate when youngmen began to talk freely of revolution and the liberation of India.

Savarkar's main aim was to infuse the youngmen whom he had gathered round with revolutionary ideas, and to involve them in revolutionary activities. He strongly believed that it was unthinkable that anything could come about by peaceful argument; and the ruling power would surrender nothing except in response to force. For building up a selfless and fearless cadre of revolutionaries, he evoked admiration for India's heritage, and antipathy for British rule which had subjected millions of people in India to untold suffering and indignities. The theme which he selected for rousing national consciousness was the struggle of 1857 which he called the First War of Indian Independence. 10 May 1907 was the fiftieth aniversary of the Revolt of 1857; and Savarkar had completed his book *The Indian War of Independence, 1857* on this occasion. Originally written in Marathi, this work was translated into English under the supervision of V.V.S. Aiyar, but no one was willing to print it in English because of its hostile indictment of British rule, and it was in Holland that a printing press was persuaded to print it, and the work finally appeared on 10 May 1909.[26]

It is not intended here to discuss Savarkar as a historian but to understand his motive in writing this book, and the nature of the impact it produced on the mind of revolutionaries. What was Savarkar's object in writing this work? For one thing, the theme of the Indian War of Independence (1857) greatly fascinated him. He believed that the history of the 1857 struggle had not been written in a truly scientific manner—the British had given their version in a "wicked and partial spirit."[27] Savarkar wanted to fill this gap in historical studies, but this scholastic urge does not explain his purpose. He regarded the episode of 1857 as a unique event of great magnitude. He wrote: "It is difficult to find in Indian history another Revolution so exciting, so exacting, so quick, so terrible, and so universal."[28] Basing his work largely on English sources readily available at the British Museum, he showed that in their war against the British, the Indian leaders of 1857 were inspired by the great principles of *Swadharma* and *Swaraj*;[29] and it was the nobility of such lofty ideals which really ought to determine the character of the entire national war. He wanted to use on a grand scale this great and meaningful episode for political reasons. The primary need of the time, according to Savarkar, was to educate his countrymen in the theory and practice of revolution, and to inspire them with the spirit of patriotism and self-sacrifice; and there was no theme other than the War of 1857 which could help him illuminate and expound so graphically and so effectively amongst his countrymen, the admirable qualities of fighting, and dying for one's country, and which could exercise also such a tremendous appeal to his countrymen. In his Introduction, he wrote:

> The nation that has no consciousness of its past has no future. Equally true it is that a nation must develop its capacity not only of claiming a past but also of knowing how to use it for the furtherance of its future.[30]

Savarkar believed in that type of history which studied the past with reference to the present. History was not a story full of sound and fury, signifying nothing, but philosophy teaching by example, and possessing the moral purpose of giving lessons to people in their adversity. His history is essentially an ideological polemic which is underpinned by copious documentation and coherent and lucid exposition. At times in the text passages overlap, thus the continuity and easy flow of the story is interrupted.

Savarkar presented a vivid and glowing portrait-gallery of heroic men who died for the love of their country; and this noble example of self-sacrifice, he wanted his followers to emulate in their fight for the liberation of their country. By using his imaginative gifts, he produced the living biographies of Indian heroes like Nana Sahib, Tatia Tope, and Lakshami Bai, and evoked in the reader's mind immense veneration for their patriotism, courage, and selflessness. He also showed how treachery, impulsiveness, petty-mindedness, and lack of coordination among leaders had destroyed their mission of liberation. The leaders, according to Savarkar, were not mutineers but freedom fighters, and the entire struggle was neither a mutiny, nor a revolt but a War of Independence in which people of all types, and from different areas, irrespective of caste and religion, plunged themselves. But the most striking feature of the whole work is Savarkar's stirring appeal to his followers and to his readers to follow their heroes, and continue their struggle; and there are many such passages of Savarkar's fierce appeal made in Carlyle's rhetorical style, a transcript of his thoughts. It might be useful to reproduce some of these passages in order to emphasize how he was deeply concerned with the past to draw lessons from it for his countrymen, particularly his followers.

Explaining how one "native state" after another was swallowed up by Lord Dalhousie's policy of comprehensive annexations, Savarkar, when he came to Satara, paused and then with a rhetorical flourish recalled the past glory of Satara in the following terms:

> The Gadi of Satara! The same Gadi on which Shivaji was crowned by the hand of Gaga Bhatt! The same Gadi to which Baji Rao I dedicated all his triumph, before which he bowed low! O Maharashtra! behold that same Gadi on which Shivaji sat, and to which homage was paid by Santaji, Bhanaji, Niraji and Baji, has been broken to pieces by Dalhousie....[31]

Savarkar compared the heroes of 1857, Nana Sahib and Lakshmi

Bai, with the fiery and intrepid Akalis of his day who were determined to "avenge their country's unjust wrongs with the last drop of their blood."[32] Savarkar made this reference to Akalis deliberately with the intention of enlisting the support of the Sikh community in the national struggle. Describing how the British policy of systematic though subtle interference in the religious practices of Hindus and Muslims caused widespread rebellion among sepoys, Savarkar wrote:

> Rise, then, O Hindustan, rise! Even as Shri Ramdas exhorted "Die for Dharma, while killing all your enemies and win back Swarajya, while killing, kill well"; Murmuring such sentiments to himself, every sepoy in India began to sharpen his sword for the fight for Swadharma and Swarajya.[33]

Chapter VI of his history entitled "Lit up the Sacrificial Fire" which is replete with the shining examples of Indian valour, and with his passionate appeals to Indians to gird up their loins, and fight the British opens on the following moving note:

> It is then inevitable that we must resist sword in hand and wage a relentless struggle to win back our political independence and to safeguard the honour of the ashes of our fathers and the temples of our gods. We must hence hasten fast to propitiate the God of War, the Lord of Hosts, even as Indrajit did before he marched on to the battlefield.... But our cause is just, is righteous! we need not fear frustration. Even though we know how to fight for what we call Right does not unfailingly win through its inherent justificability or righteousness unless and until it is upheld by proportionate Might, even then to fight for our Right to the best of our might is in itself a heroic joy which fills the warrior with a divine intoxication.[34]

As in the above passage, Savarkar expressed in his work at quite a number of places his immense faith in the use of violence for political ends; for example, he warned that "all attempts to win back the country and its independence by conciliation and money, and by appeal had so far failed; hence be ready for war." Reminding his countrymen that they ought to follow the noble example of their heroes, he declared eloquently: "Mangal Pandey is gone but his spirit has spread all over Hindustan. The principle for which he fought has become immortal. Let every mother teach her son the story of this hero with pride."[35] Savarkar reiterated that India was vital, sensitive, and ready to face any challenge; for example, he warned, "The days are gone when India would don other people's caps. Throw away their slavish caps."[36] He greatly admired the lofty glories of the 1857 leaders, but lamented the boisterous imbecility of the populace to meet the challenge. History with Savarkar was not only a story of victory and of heroic grandeur, but of defeat of downright treachery, and selfish fury, also. In the following passage, he recognized the urgency of examining the whole episode from the angles of both the victor and the vanquished:

> Tell us now, O Muse of History, how Nana Sahib, the Moulvie of Lucknow, the Ranee of Jhansi, and other grand heroes clung to their principle with such extra-ordinary persistence! And fail not to tell, also O history how all Indians could not cling to it as these heroes did! Come and sing the songs of glory and of praise with us in the first part, and, also come and weep with us later on.[37]

Savarkar provided in his narrative a host of maxims pithy and meaningful to his countrymen; for example, he did not believe in the philosophy of "forget and forgive" but declared: "For every Englishman, a whole village had been burnt, God will not forget this and we will never forget this."[38] His condemnation of the servility of his countrymen is evident in the following comment: "How many cowardly Hindus are there not in India who are harmless and cringing when trodden under foot by the English."[39] At times a feeling of dismay and remorse overpowered him, particularly when he thought of the crushing slavery weighing down India. He addressed the Ganges in dismay, "Oh! Ganges how many more of the impure loads you have to carry before you send them to their ocean home."[40] As a pious Hindu he concluded his version of the Cawnpore massacre with the prayer that "Mother Ganges, who drank that day of the blood of Europeans, may drink her fill of it again."[41] He believed in the principle that the life of an individual was of little consequence as compared with that of a nation; he wrote: "Individuals, peasants or kings—may live or die but the nation should not die."[42] According to Savarkar, dying for one's country was a glorious act, a performence of the highest form of duty. In this context he stated: "These that are so brave and so self-sacrificing get, if not the Bahadur Shah medal, yet the nobler ones, the Duty medal of Martyrdom, even from the hands of death himself."[43] At another place when he narrated the fall of Lucknow, he wrote:

> But, fear could exist only in the hearts of ordinary mortals. Those who, charmed by the ideal of independence, welcomed death as the only means of achieving the ideal—who could succeed in frightening these? Who fights for victory fears; who battles for glory, even, may fear; but who could frighten him who fights for death alone? The utmost one can be afraid of is death! But he who has overstepped those limits, and who smiles on death what could frighten him? What could come in the way of such a man? Not all the thunders and all the lightenings of dread heaven could stop his progress; for his progress is towards death and those elements are only rendering his task easier. He who hopes for death alone has no room for despair. These national heroes of Itawah who courted death in battle with the ardour of a lover for his love, what could frighten them, then?[44]

At moments Savarkar's work is interpersed with reflections on his philosophy of life; for him life was a continuous battle in so far it was an entity at all. His image of the elephant breaking his tusk, and trying to smash a mountain[45] represented collision with Difficulty and Necessity, and was like walking which is a series of falls. But he urged that the fire of inner-self must be kept burning; for example, he wrote: "The sacred fuel burning in the sacrificial fire is a thousand times more life-giving than the log of wood burning in the funeral pyre."[46] He believed that the sacrifices by martyrs in 1857 had not been in vain because they were bound to influence the future course of events. Savarkar prayed, "Let your blood and bravery purify the Past and incite and inspire the Future."[47] According to him, martyrs never die, they continue to live, enshrined in the hearts of people, and he addressed these martyrs, "May my country learn from your death at least the lesson that soldiers who fight to live, die and that those who fight to die, live."[48] He strongly urged his countrymen to continue the fight waged in 1857 which must be carefully planned, avoiding the blunders committed earlier in planning and organization. No war, according to Savarkar, could be waged without stern discipline, and complete sacrifice, "calmness in preparation, but boldness in execution," this should be the watchwords, he added.[49] Though Bahadur Shah does not emerge as a man of action, yet at the end of his work, Savarkar portrayed him as a sensitive poet dedicated to the cause of the independence of his country. Savarkar concludes:

> Emperor Bahadur Shah was a poet. During the heart of the Revolution he composed a *Gazal*. Some one asked him:
> *Dumdumaymen dam nahin khair mango janki*
> *Ai Zafar thandi hui Shamsher Hindustanki*
> (Now that, every moment, you are becoming weaker, pray for your life [to the English]: for, Oh! Emperor, the sword of India is now broken for ever!)
> There is a tradition that the Emperor replied:
> *Ghazionmen bu rahegi jabtalak imanki*
> *Tabto Londontak chalegi teg Hindustanki.*
> (As long as there remains the least trace of love of faith in the hearts of our heroes, so long, the sword of Hindustan shall be sharp, and one day shall flash even at the gates of London.)[50]

It seems as though in accordance with the wishes of Bahadur Shah, Savarkar was sharpening his weapons in London for waging a relentless battle with the British between 1906-09.

Savarkar's *War of Independence* became almost a Bible for the revolutionaries at India House, a *vade-macum* in the ideology of Revolution. By early 1907, Savarkar had prepared the manuscript of this work; and since then at weekly meetings in India House, he read out some of its portions to his followers in inimitable eloquence. His History provoked lively and heated discussions among his followers—there was often a raising of arms, and thumping of tables. At one meeting in India House, presided over by Miranjan, a law student from Maharashtra and attended by twenty-five persons on 4 April 1909, Aiyer read about 100 pages from Savarkar's manuscript; and when in the portion dealing with the revolt of Oudh Bahadur Shah's name was mentioned, the "entire audience stood up, cheered, and yelled in a most enthusiastic manner."[51]

A regular feature of the India House activities was the annual celebration of Martyrs Day on 10 May, the anniversary of the War of Independence (1857). The idea of celebrating this day was initiated not by Savarkar but by Krishnavarma on 10 May 1905. The first commemoration of the Mutiny took the form of a dinner in honour of Krishnavarma at an Indian restaurant, Shaftsbury Avenue. The function was presided over by the extremist barrister J.M. Parikh. At this meeting Dr Pereira remarked that "it was only by blood that India could be freed."[52] The following is a copy of the invitation card printed in red, and issued on the occasion.[53]

Bande Mataram.
To commemorate the aniversary of
The
INDIAN NATIONAL RISING
of 1857
A MEETING OF INDIANS IN
ENGLAND
will be held at
INDIA HOUSE
65, Cromwell Avenue, Highgate N.
on Sunday the 10th of May, 1908,
at 4 P.M. precisely.

You and all your Indian friends are cordially invited to be present.

The fiftieth anniversary of this historic day was celebrated in India House on 10 May 1907 with great elan under the direction of Savarkar. On this annual day, which brought together Indian students to India House from different parts of England, there were scenes of frenzied argument, of frothy eloquence—and of the distribution of colourful Martyr badges.

Savarkar had produced for the use of his followers another patriotic work entitled *Joseph Mazzini: His Autobiography and Politics*,[54] a Marathi version of the life of Mazzini with an eloquent introduction elevating politics to the sphere of religion. He had dedicated it to Tilak and S.M. Paranjpe. This work is largely based on the six volumes of Mazzini's writings. Why did Savarkar think it necessary to present Mazzini's biography to his countrymen? What was the real motive? For one thing, Savarkar saw in Mazzini the fighter against desperate odds, the patriot, and the champion of the oppressed. For another, he thought that under the guise of Mazzini's speeches and writings, he could easily disseminate his revolutionary ideas among his countrymen without the possibility of his being implicated by the British government on the charge of revolutionary activities. It was a tactical move on his part to achieve the desired results.

According to Savarkar, the problems of India were similar to the problems of Mazzini's Italy, so Savarkar exhorted his compatriots to draw lessons from Mazzini's life, and wage their struggle accordingly. His study showed that Italy could never achieve her object without resorting to the armed struggle.[55] He justified fighting provided the cause was virtuous. This edition (of 200 copies) strongly urged the need for procuring and storing of weapons from neighbouring countries as Italy had done in her struggle against Austria, and using them when the occasion demanded.[56] There is a significant passage in Savarkar's Introduction which provides a key to the understanding of the entire purpose underlying this work. Savarkar, while dilating upon Mazzini's programme of instruction and war, wrote:

> The suggested methods of preparation for war are the purchase and storing of weapons in neighbouring countries to be used when opportunity should occur, the opening of many very small but secret factories at some distance from one another, for the manufacture of weapons clandestinely in the country seeking Independence, and the purchase by secret societies of weapons in other countries to be secretly imported in merchant ships.[57]

Savarkar also acquired proficiency in the Gurmukhi language which he intended to use for the study of the *Adi Granth*. His publication *O Martyrs* in which he made a strong appeal to his countrymen gained wide circulation among Indian youth, and was issued later as a pamphlet.[58] On the occasion of the 50th anniversary of the Revolt of 1857 which was called the annual Martyrs Day, Savarkar read out this appeal to about 100 students some of whom had travelled from Oxford, Cambridge, and even from Edinburgh to attend the function. Savarkar's eloquence made a great impression, and the programme lasted about four hours. *The Times* reported that the students taking the vow to dedicate themselves to the cause of India's liberation were given badges to commemorate their commitment.[59] It is not necessary to give here a summary of this eloquent Address but to emphasize that in his speech, Savarkar enjoined on his countrymen as their sacred duty to continue the war waged by the heroes of 1857 until India became free. He said:

> The War began [begun] on the 10th of May 1857 is not over on the 10th of May 1908, nor shall it ever cease till on 10th of May-to-come sees the destiny accomplished, sees the beautiful India crowned.

The Indian Sociologist, edited and published by Krishnavarma from Paris regularly every month, was read eagerly by the young revolutionaries in India House. The favourite theme of this journal was to urge the people of India to carry on their struggle against the British secretly, and to adopt the Russian methods of terrorism for produciug tangible results. The essential features of the programme recommended in the journal were: (1) the use of violence for political ends which was regarded as legitimate; (2) the maintenance of absolute secrecy in plans; and (3) the diffusion of revolutionary ideas in the army. The following extracts from the issues of *The Indian Sociologist* will suffice to give an adequate idea about the nature of the methods suggested for fighting the British.

December 1907:
> It seems that any agitation in India now must be carried on secretly, and that the only methods which can bring the English Government to its senses are the Russian methods vigorously and incessantly applied until the English relax their tyranny and are driven out of the country. No one can foresee what rule will be laid down or line of action defined for any particular course. That will probably depend on local conditions and circumstances, but it is likely that as a general principle the Russian method will begin with Indian officials rather than with European.

February 1908:
> Mr. Swinny dwells on the hopelessness of rebellion, and to judge from his use of the word "happy" he seems to gloat over "the overwhelming military force of the constituted authorities," but

he must remember that the major part of the military force is made up of Indians, and if they once see the enormity of their folly and no longer allow themselves to be tools in the hands of the cunning despotism which uses them to maintain their subjection and that of their country-men, British rule in India will end speedily and ignominiously.

April 1908:

To judge from the brutal murders of unarmed innocent Indians who recently assembled at Tinnevelly to express their joy at the release of Bepin Chandra Pal from jail and who were butchered at the instance of the British Government, the safest plan for Indians would seem to be to organise secret and determined and combined disaffection, as suggested by a European friend.

August 1908:

As to the ethics of dynamite, it may be laid down in a general way that where the people have political power there is no need for the use of explosives. It only promotes reaction. But where the people are utterly defenceless, both politically and militarily, then one may look on the bomb or any other weapon as legitimate. Its employment then becomes merely a question of expediency. We hope to discuss this question, particularly with reference to India, in an early issue of *The Indian Sociologist*.[60]

In view of the inflammable reading material supplied by *The Indian Sociologist* in its issues, the British Government was convinced that its circulation among the Indian youth was creating a strong anti-British sentiment.

Under Savarkar's leadership, the revolutionary activities gained momentum at India House, particularly at the end of 1908 and in the early months of 1909. Savarkar let no opportunity slip for rallying the forces in the cause of regenerating national sentiments. In June 1908, Dr Desai, a student of London University, delivered a lecture on "The Making of Bombs."[61] On 8 November 1908 Savarkar lectured on "Are We Really Disarmed?" and declared that there was ample war like material in India which could jeopardize British power provided the support of the Indian army and native states could be enlisted.[62] The birth centenary of Guru Gobind Singh was celebrated on 29 December 1908 at Caxton Hall, London, which was presided over by Bipan Chander Pal, and attended by about 150 persons. Lala Lajpat Rai also spoke on the occasion but the most eloquent account of the life of Gobind Singh was given by Dr Gokal Chand Narang, a specialist on Sikh History, who expounded the three tenets of Sikh political ethics, *Deg, Teg,* and *Fathe*.[63] Narang exhorted the Indian students to abandon their studies and work for the liberation of their country:

> If you are working for the bar, give it up! If you are studying engineering, give it up! Work for your country, and get money; your mother country demands still greater sacrifice of you.

Stirring songs like *Pagri Sambhal Jatha* and *O Mardana,* which were sung on the occasion, moved the audience almost to tears by their revolutionary content and emotional appeal.[64] The other leaders who spoke in the India House during 1908 were G.S. Khaparde, Har Dayal, and Ram Bhaj Dutt.[65]

The atmosphere at India House was surcharged with excitement due also to local issues which greatly concerned the young revolutionaries. The Benchers of the Inner Temple had disallowed Krishnavarma from being called to the Bar on 30 April 1909 for publishing some revolutionary articles in *The Indian Sociologist.* Such a severe action was bound to encourage the inmates of India House who protested against it vehemently at their meetings.[66] But the matter did not end there; other actions followed soon which produced widespread resentment and agony. The Benchers of the Gray's Inn had refused to call Savarkar and Harnam Singh to the Bar on account of their anti-British activities.[67] The Indian student community felt outraged at the Benchers' action which it regarded as an infringement of their legitimate rights.[68] Savarkar fumed and fretted, and poured forth his fury in his speeches. Martyrs Day was celebrated on 9 May 1909 and was presided over by Harnam Singh who had been expelled from Cirencester Agricultural College for wearing the Martyr's batch which he had refused to remove at the request of the Principal. On this occasion Savarkar assailed the Bencher's arbitrary action in disbarring him and Harnam Singh.[69] He cited specific instances how Indians including Krishnavarma were being penalized on false pretexts by the British authorities. In his passionate appeal to students to unite themselves together in this crisis, Savarkar eulogized the chivalry of Nana Sahib and the heroism of sepoys at Cawnpore who had fought against heavy odds.[70] He mentioned movingly the innocent women and babies who had been bayoneted by the British soldiery and exposed the brutality of the British repressive methods. After these historical references Savarkar came to personal issues. The immediate threat of the termination of their studies forged the bond of unity among these young students in their hostility to the British.

While the tempo of agitation was speeding up in India House, disconcerting news arrived from India. Savarkar's brother, Ganesh Savarkar, had been sentenced to transportation on life under Section 121 (Treason) and two years rigorous imprisonment under Section 124 (Sedition). Ganesh had been punished for publishing and distributing revolutionary pamphlets which had been sent by Vinayak for the *Mitra Mela*.[71]

This news of his brother's arrest threw Savarkar in a proxyism of rage, and he was beside himself. His tone became violent, and in his speech on 20 June 1909 at India House he declared that he would not rest until he wreaked vengeance on the British for unleashing oppressive forces both in India and England.[72] He learnt also about his mentor Tilak's arrest for producing seditionary literature and this wounded him. Further, there was news about Khudi Ram Bose's killing two English women, and his glorious sacrifice in facing the gallows. All these factors, both personal and national, infuriated Savarkar and his followers; they felt humiliated and embittered at the Benchers' action, and outraged at Ganesh and Tilak's arrests, and Khudi Ram Bose's execution. The only way to release these pent-up feelings was to take revenge upon the British for the wrongs done to their countrymen. This they thought was the only course left to them. A valuable eye-witness report on Savarkar and India House at this period has been given by David Garnet who was gifted with artistic sensibility combined with exquisite narrative power. Savarkar provides a sensitive portrait:

> He was small, slight in build, with very broad cheekbones, a delicate equiline nose, a sensitive refined mouth and an extremely pale skin which was almost as pale as ivory on the forehead and cheekbones but darker in the hollows.[73]

Garnet attended one of the meetings at India House of which he gives graphic details:

Savarkar after my arrival was trooped into the dining room and Savarkar after addressing the company in Hindi, stood up and began to read aloud. As I could not understand what he was reading, I looked about the room without paying much attention to him. The sight of those brown men, some sitting round a long table and others leaning against the wall all listening to the staccato voice of the speaker was very strange to me. At the meeting I felt alone. ... But the consciousness of this gulf did not dismay me.[74]

About the type of people assembled whom Garnet described as "lively boys and obese men," he adds:

Meanwhile, how strange they looked; one older man near me was bearded and wore a fez; the others were bare-headed with their black, oily ringlets and black eyes; some speaking with fun and life, others like dry, black olives. And looking at them, it was not impossible to classify them as higher and lower racial types, and judging them physically by European standards. There were those with sensitive, delicate features and, those with coarse negroid lips, Aryans and Dravadian perhaps.[75]

But it was Savarkar who really dominated the scene, and who was reading out portions from his *War of Independence:* Garnet continues his narrative:

Then I looked at Savarkar and thought his was the most sensitive face in the room and yet the most powerful. I watched how he spat out his words, with almost convulsive movements. And, from looking at him, I became aware that he was reading aloud in English not in Hindustani. His accent, his mispronunciations, the strange rhythm of his staccato delivery had deceived me. What a wool-gathering fool I was! But it was a relief to have made the discovery for myself. I listened then attentively and made out that he was reading about a battle in which an Indian General called Tatia Tope had been defeated by English troops and Sikhs.

Savarkar was, although I did not know it, reading aloud a chapter from his extremely propagandist history of the Indian Mutiny called The Indian War of Independence of 1857 by an Indian

Nationalist which was secretly printed a few months later. When he had finished his chapter, the greater part of the audience went to an adjoining room. . . .[76]

Garnet waxes lyrical on Savarkar and his transparent sincerity in the following words:

> I saw a certain amount of Savarkar and was more than ever struck by his extraordinary personal magneticism. There was an intensity of faith in the man and a curious single-minded restlessness which was deeply attractive to me.[77]

Savarkar was so deeply absorbed in his work that he was completely "indifferent to filth and oblivious to his environment." The India House had also its lighter side, fun, wit and music. Garnet touches on the social aspect. "A woman was singing in a high falsetto voice.... For the first time I realised that there were Hindu women as well as lively boys and obese men."[78]

One of the favourite songs usually sung was *Bande Mataram*, an Indian hymn which was proscribed at that time. In fact, among the inmates of India House these two words *Bande Mataram* were used in greeting and salute the same way as the Nazis used *Heil Hitler*.

The British were not indifferent to the political activities in India House, and kept a close vigilance on them. The Scotland Yard had planted informers in India House with the object of ferreting out information about the revolutionaries. Garnet reports that on his visit to India House his friends said that the man assigned to be sentinel for the meeting and known to be an informer was posted outside in the garden so that he could not report on what was happening inside.[79]

The young revolutionaries at India House were not idle intellectuals spinning miles of words, eloquent only in their speeches, and hysterical in their gesticulations. They had realized that neither petitions nor appeals to the British were likely to produce any results; only violent means would force the British in yielding concessions to the legitimate demands of Indians. Therefore, they were determined to do something definite. They were young, somewhat raw, passionate in their zeal, fixed in their convictions, mercurial at times, swayed by emotions but radical in their outlook; they were always in a hurry. Nor encumbered by financial cares, free to do what they liked because of the lack of parental control, they developed a close fraternity, an *esprit de corps*. Savarkar cast his spell on those round him by the force of his magnetic personality; his jaw struck terror, and his handshake could convert others to his ideology,[80] and he would administer in secrecy an oath to his followers binding them in commitment to his plans. This is not to suggest that each of those who were closely associated with him in his programme turned a puppet to delight Savarkar's whim and caprice; each one responded according to his inclination of mind which was conditioned by the nature and circumstances of the situation.

These youngmen, influenced by the revolutionary propaganda, were carried away with the notion of resorting to some violent type of action against the British. Savarkar had made arrangements for the training of his followers in revolver-training centre at Tottenhem Court Road, London, run by John S. Morley of "Fun Land"; and had deputed his confident Govind Amin to supervise the arrangements.[81] He obtained a manual on bomb-making from Russian revolutionaries through Hem Chandra Dass and distributed its cyclostyled copies among his followers, and sent some of them to his brother Ganesh in India.[82] In those days his hands bore the stains of picric acid—he was busy experimenting the manufacture of bombs. He had acquired in February 1909 a parcel of twenty Browning pistols with ammunition from Paris through Amin who served as a cook at India House, and sent them out to Bombay for "anarchical purposes."[83] Bapat had learnt the bomb-manufacture formula in 1919, and wanted to blow the House of Parliament, but Savarkar advised restraint saying:

> There will no doubt be thunder and lightening in the darkness of our present condition. But what of the deadlier darkness that will descend on our mission? It will be more profitable to disseminate this art of bomb-making through our different branches of the Abhinav Bharat and equip them with a weapon which is more effective.[84]

Meanwhile all through these years from 1906 when Madan Lal Dhingra came to England, he was closely associated with India House and its activities. Shy and reserved, he seldom spoke at India

House meetings but there was hardly a meeting he missed. According to the Criminal Intelligence Report, he "did not appear to have taken any prominent part in the Indian agitation in India."[85] Not everyone is supposed to come to the fore in political or revolutionary campaign, but Savarkar possessed an uncanny but sure instinct of recognizing individual talent, and utilizing it to the best advantage. He knew that Dhingra was of shy temperament, and that his talents could be employed better in the background.

Dhingra was present at the first meeting of the Abhinav Bharat at the residence of Nitisen Das under the Chairmanship of Ali Khan.[86] He was a resident of India House in May 1907 for about a month when Savarkar, Bapat, and G.C. Varma were also staying there.[87] He resided again in India House for six months from March or April 1908, and for another month in April 1909 until he shifted to 108 Ledbury Road, Bayswater, W. where he lived on the ground floor, paid 15 shilling a week with partial Board; usually went out between 11 and 12, and returned mostly at 7 P.M. and stayed thereafter home. In April 1909 the anti-British campaign had reached its peak in India House, and Dhingra who resided there was asked by his parents to vacate it, and shift elsewhere. Though he shifted to Ledbury Road, his interest in India House never flagged. David Garnet had met Dhingra once in India House, and called him a "Byronic young man" who smiled and walked briskly, and who had "stopped the Harry Lander record at his request."[88] Dhingra was present at the meeting on 24 January 1909, and on 26 February when one Naidu read a paper on "How a nationalist views the appointment of the Indian law member."[89] A report shows him leaving India House in company with Savarkar and nine others; he had also brought in his brother Bhajan Lal Dhingra to attend the meeting when Savarkar and Koregaonkar spoke violently against the Benchers' decisions to impose restrictions on Savarkar and Harnam Singh.[90]

Thus in this developing revolutionary campaign against the British by Indians there was a leader in Savarkar, an ideology in militant nationalism, and a team of followers in the members of Abhinav Bharat and others connected with India House. But who was to be the target, and what was to be the means?

The Director, Intelligence, C.J. Stevenson-Moore, in his letter to the Commissioner of Police, London, had anticipated that the "outrage will be committed in London."[91] Here was some unusual prognostication!

3 The Assassination

Sir William Curzon Wyllie was shot on 1 July 1909, about 11 P.M. in the Institute of Imperial Studies, London. A young man crouching with a revolver in hand fired two shots in quick succession followed by two others, and Sir Curzon dropped dead. After a short interval, two more shots were fired when Dr Cawas Lalcaca tried to save Sir Curzon, but he too fell down, receiving serious injuries. The youngman was overpowered, and gave his name as "Dhingra."

Sir Curzon was the Political Aide-de-camp to the Secretary of State for India, Lord Morley.[1] His father General Sir William Wyllie G.C.B. had served with distinction in the First Afghan War, 1838-40. Born in 1848, Curzon Wyllie had joined the Indian Staff Corpse (later called the Indian Army) in 1869, was selected for service in the Oudh Commission in 1870, and joined the Political Department of the Government of India in 1879. During the Afghan War (1879-80) he served under Sir Robert Sandeman and was attached to General Phyare's force for the relief of Kandhar. He was Military Secretary to Adam, Governor of Madras, but on Adam's death, was Private Secretary to Hudelston, the Acting Governor. He was employed in the Indian states—notably Hyderabad and in other states of Central India. He was also Resident in Nepal in 1898, Agent to the Governor-General in Rajputana in 1899, and Chief Commissioner Ajmer-Merwar in the Foreign Department of India in 1901 when he was appointed the Political Aide-de-camp to the Secretary of State for India. He received the C.I.E in 1881, K.C.I.E. in September 1902, the M.V.O. in August of the same year, and was appointed C.V.O. in January 1907. He was married to the daughter of D.E. Carmichael, Chief Secretary, 1877, and Member of Council, 1878-83, and an associate of Sir Mounstuart Grant Duff, the Governor of Madras.[2]

Sir William Curzon Wyllie
(India Office Library, London)

The Assassination

Dr Cawas Khurshedji Lalcaca, whom Dhingra also had shot down, was a prominent medical practitioner from Shanghai. Originally belonging to a highly educated Parsi family of Bombay, he had settled in Shanghai, and established a lucrative practice and high social position. He seldom mixed with the members of his own community; and when a riot broke out in Shanghai between the Chinese and White population, his car was set on fire because he was known to be a pronounced pro-European. He narrowly escaped in this affray. A bachelor about forty-eight, with dark complexion and striking pointed beard, he had come to England for a pleasure trip during the summer, and had been in London since 8 June 1909.[3]

The National Indian Association, primarily a Social Forum meant for introducing Indians to each other, and to other visitors, especially to the sympathetic English, was holding on 1 July 1909 one of its several evening gatherings in the Imperial Institute, London, arranged in the course of the year. On such occasions a fairly large number of people were invited including British officials and retired civil servants, and were entertained with a variety programme. Sir Charles Lyall, formerly Chief Commissioner, Central Provinces, 1895-98, and Secretary at the Indian Office in the Judicial and Public Department, 1898, and Lady Lyall were receiving the guests who had started pouring in from 9 P.M. and about 200 people had assembled. But Sir William Curzon Wyllie and Lady Wyllie had arrived late, at about 10.30 P.M. They had been held up in Savoy Hotel where they were dining with their old friend, Fazulboy Currimbhoy Ebrahim of the Bombay Mill Owners' Association, and his brother. After their dinner, they arrived at the function of the National Indian Association where the musical items were being given in the Jehangir Hall in the Imperial Institute.

By 11 P.M. the stream of departures set in, and people being in cheerful mood, said good-bye to each other after a pleasant evening at which they had enjoyed some music and light refreshments. Nobody could imagine that this fun and merry-making would change into a grim tragedy in so short a time!

Sir Curzon was leaving the main Jehangir Hall above the ground floor. He was seen talking to a young man; what passed between them was not audible. Lady Wyllie had been escorted to the cloak room downstairs by Ebrahim. Sir Curzon had stopped to talk to one or two Indians, and he had just passed through the folding door of the Hall. He entered the large landing outside, some portions of which were screened from the stairs. Just two yards away from the stairs Dhingra engaged him in conversation and they were a yard apart from each other.[4] Dhingra then placed the muzzle close to Sir Curzon's face and fired four shots. One bullet shattered Curzon's right eye, and another bullet pierced his face below the left eye. As Wyllie fell, Dhingra fired another shot at Dr Lalcaca who had reached forward to save Wyllie; he too fell down, died on the way to St. George Hospital.[5]

Three fairly accurate and informative eye-witness accounts of how Dhingra fired at Sir Curzon Wyllie and Dr Lalcaca are given in the Trial proceedings. The first account is by Madan Mohan Sinha, a young law student from the Middle Temple, who said:

I saw a man with a revolver in his right hand. He was facing towards the steps and Wyllie was facing him. I saw the man actually fire at Sir Curzon. I saw the flash, a puff of smoke, and the deceased fell. . . . The shot aimed at the left side of Wyllie's face. Wyllie dropped. I rushed to save him. More than four shots were fired in quick succession.[6]

Douglas William Thorburn, a journalist, who also witnessed the firing, corroborated Sinha's version in his statement which is as follows:

I looked to the vestibule. I could see very few people round the door, could see only two people in the vestibule. One was Wyllie and the other a youngman in lounge suit, and blue turban, facing one another, at arms length, apparently conversing. As I saw the prisoner raise his arm, I saw a revolver and he fired four shots in the face of Wyllie who fell on the ground—more shots were fired after an interval of a few seconds. I saw the flash.[7]

Sir Leslie Probyn, a close friend of Sir Curzon Wyllie, gave the following vivid and moving account of the sombre tragedy:

I heard sounds as of shots three or four fired rapidly. Then I went forward and heard another and then I saw another one fired. I suppose I must have gone through the exit down after the first three or four shots. Curzon was three or four yards from the door in the vestibule. I heard shots about two yards or less away from Curzon; he was firing at the left side from the neck upwards. The puff of the smoke went that way. Curzon's head moved from one side to the other and he dropped three or four yards from the door.[8]

After Dhingra had fired at Dr Lalcaca, he stood holding the revolver in his hand. Fear and panic had seized the guests who had witnessed the brutal scene in utter helplessness. Dhingra might leap forward and fire again. Meanwhile two persons closed in on Dhingra from opposite directions. Madan Mohan Sinha rushed to him and pulled him down from the back. Sinha said: "I got to his back and holding his arms pushed him against some chairs causing him to lose his balance and he fell. I held him down with my knee on his back until the police came."[9]

Sir Leslie had to struggle hard in his encounter with Dhingra, and received some minor injuries, but ultimately succeeded in overpowering him. In his statement, he said that after rushing at Dhingra

I caught hold of his left hand with my right [illegible]. And then I never let go of his left hand and I managed to get the revolver into my left hand. I suppose I tumbled down somehow but I never let go the revolver. I suppose the prisoner resisted. I do not know. I tumbled on my nose and injured my ribs and my face. My nose bled. After a while after the struggle was over, the police arrived.[10]

Giving more details as how Sir Leslie handled Dhingra and put him on the defensive, he said:

I heard four shots in quick succession, pushed him with my right knee. He fell over by some chairs on to his knees. I was still holding him from the back with my right knee on his back. He had the pistol in his hand and was struggling hard. There were other people fighting in front of him. I held him and shouted for help. I held him till the police came.[11]

Dhingra was thus encircled and overpowered by Sinha, and a little later by Sir Leslie who was assisted by Thorburn. At first, Dhingra had levelled his pistol at Sinha but immediately he put the muzzle of the revolver on his right temple, the revolver clicked but there was no explosion. He attempted to shoot himself but he had used up all the bullets. He wanted to take his own life in order to evade the terrible ordeal that lay ahead on the arrest, the ignomony, the harassment, the trial and execution with all its grisly accompaniment.

After Dhingra was subdued, he was seated on a chair, and four or five persons were holding him. All the eyes were fixed on him. It was an ordeal for him, or for anyone in that situation, to be a centre of so much public gaze. By and large, the general feeling for him would have been one of utter contempt, and for Lady Curzon Wyllie, spontaneous sympathy. Dr Lalcaca had been removed to the hospital, and Sir Curzon's dead body was lying nearby; and Lady Curzon, broken in spirit, was sobbing—the only sound audible in the otherwise atmosphere of pin-drop silence. It was absolutely quite and tense. Dhingra was staring in the empty space then, a habit of mind which people indulge in when they have nothing to think, nothing to feel—a state of utter insensitivity, both of mind and feeling. But why should he think, feel, or say anything? His mission was over, and whatever he had wanted to achieve, he had achieved. There was no regret, no fear, and no qualms of conscience to disturb him. The deed was done.

Dhingra was asked a number of questions by people surrounding him, but he was in no mood to answer them. He just ignored them as if they had not been asked. But when Rolleston asked him his name, he gave it as "Dhingra."[12] Thorburn, the journalist, pressed him to answer "Why have you done it or something to that effect," but he looked quietly into his face, and said nothing. Charles Rolleston would not leave the matter there, and asked him further his motive to which Dhingra said that he would tell the police what he had to say. He believed that it was none of his business to tell them, and none of their business to know. All these moments, when he was subjected to a volley of irritating questions in the presence of such a large number of people who had little sympathy for him, must have been intensely painful; probably a more painful ordeal than when he had been making up his mind to fire. The moment of preparation is warming up, but when the deed is over, it is all

The Assassination

cold, a torrential release of the arrested and long stored up resolves, conflicts, and passions. In the melee when he was being hemmed in, his turban and glasses fell, and the only thing he said was "my specs," which were given to him. But from all the eye-witness accounts, it is clear beyond doubt that he was the calmest of persons, "the only person not agitated or excited."[13] It seemed as though his head was packed in ice. When someone asked whether he would like his friends or relatives to be informed, he just kept silent. In the meanwhile, the police arrived, and people pointing to him said that this was the man who did it.

The first thing that the police did was to search Dhingra while he was being held by four or five persons, and in this task, they were assisted by Charles Rolleston, a retired army officer, Fredrick Nicholas, a police officer, and Madan Mohan Sinha. They found in his right hand, inside great pocket a small revolver (a six chamber fully loaded), a dagger in a leather case, a roll of papers, a number of small slips of paper, a pen-knife, few keys, some money about six or seven shillings, a pair of spectacles in a case, several loose keys, a handkerchief, and a pair of glasses. They recovered from his lodgings a picture postcard of the original painting of the great Russian painter Verastchagin depicting the blowing off Indian rebels from the muzzles of field gun in India, 1857-58, and the other a portrait of Lord Curzon on which was pencilled "Heathen Dog."[14]

The police took Dhingra under their custody, and removed him to Brixton jail. He was subjected to severe cross-examination, but he answered the interrogations with a smile.[15] When Albert Draper, the Detective-Inspector, enquired whether he would wish any of his friends to be "communicated with," he replied, "I do not think it necessary to-night but they will know it later on."[16] He regretted Dr Lalcaca's death, and made a statement about it to Albert Draper:

> The only thing that I want to say is that there was no wilful murder in the case of Dr. Lalcaca. I did not know him. When he advanced to get hold of me, I simply fired in self-defence.[17]

Those who met him in jail found him absolutely calm and steady; he was wearing a striped lounge suit with gold-rimmed spectacles, minus a tie and laces which were removed to prevent any attempt on his part to commit suicide.[18] But about Sir Curzon Wyllie, he felt no remorse, he wanted to kill him, and so he did it. It was just that.

After Dhingra's arrest there was considerable activity among his friends and associates in India House who greatly admired his act but were now deeply concerned about the impending fate that lay in store for their beloved companion. According to the report of the Scottland Yard, they were anxious to offer defence and give him a solicitor, and for this purpose, they approached him. Dr T.S. Rajan, and later, H.K. Koregaonkar met him in jail in this connection, but Dhingra turned down the suggestion.[19] Savarkar and Koregaonkar visited Dhingra on 23 July, and had an interview with him of a quarter of an hour's duration, and it is probable that Savarkar too tried to persuade him to put up a defence. V.V.S. Aiyer too associated himself with Dr Rajan and Koregaonkar's idea of engaging a solicitor for Dhingra, and tried to bring him round.[20] G.S. Khaparde, who lived in London those days, noted in his diary that Dr Pollen went to Dhingra in prison with an offer to defend him *gratis* but Dhingra refused.[21] Dhingra also received several sympathetic letters from Indians living in England on the same subject but he was determined not to offer any defence. On the contrary, he found his action morally right, and he decided to justify it.

Dhingra was convinced that what he had done was just the right thing to do, and that he would do it over again if another such opportunity were ever offered to him—remorse, regret, or compunction he had none, whatsoever. He believed that neither the British Court of Justice, nor British public opinion nor even the leaders of Indian opinion who condemned the use of violence for political ends could really judge his act dispassionately—his real judge in a matter like this which involved higher justice was his own conscience, and some of his close associates in India House like Savarkar, Koregaonkar, Harnam Singh, and others, who had organized the Brotherhood-in arms against the British regime in India. His own family also wanted to engage a solicitor for him, but Dhingra rejected this move; he even refused to see his brother Bhajan Lal, who visited the prison for this purpose.

Some of his friends who met Dhingra in prison found him in high spirits. When Charles Glass, the Sub-Divisional Inspector, read out the charges of wilful murder against him, Dhingra nodded his head, and replied "yes."[22] He was, as usual, very reserved in

The Assassination

the court. Ilbert Issac, Superintendent of Bench Divison, stated that on hearing the charges, Dhingra simply nodded his head, his lips moved, but what he said was inaudible.[23] At one time, he is reported to have raised his head in the court, and said, softly, though firmly, "you can pass sentence of death on me. You are all powerful and do what you like. But remember, we shall have our time."[24] On another occasion, he saluted in a military fashion in the court, and addressed the judge, "Thank you, my lord, I am glad to have the honour of dying for my countrymen."[25] Four days before he was hanged, he appeared in the court, and saluted in the same military fashion, repeating almost the same declaration. "I thank you, my lord, I am prepared to lay down my life. It is a great honour."[26]

On 10 July, Dhingra was asked whether he wished to say anything in answer to the charges, and he read out the following statement:

> I do not want to say anything in defence of myself, but simply to prove the justice of my deed. As for myself I do not think that any English law court has any authority to convict me or detain me in prison or to pass sentence of death to me.
>
> That is the reason I did not have any counsel to defend me. And I maintain that if it is patriotic in an Englishman to fight against the Germans if they were to occupy this country, it is much more justifiable and patriotic in my case to fight against the English; I hold the English people responsible for the murder of eighty millions of my countrymen, Indians, I mean, in the last fifty years. And they are also responsible for taking away £100,000,000 every year from India to this country. I also hold them responsible for the hanging and deportations of my countrymen, who do just the same as the English people here are advising their countrymen to do; and an Englishman who goes out to India, and say, gets £100 a month, that simply means that he passes sentence of death on 1,000 of my poor countrymen. Because these 4000 people can easily live with those £100 which the Englishmen spend mostly in his frivolities and pleasures. Just as Germans have no right to occupy their country, so the English people have no right to occupy India, and it is perfectly justifiable on our part to kill an Englishman who is polluting our sacred land. I am surprised at the terrible hypo-

cricy, force and mockery of the English people, when they pose as champions of oppressed humanity—as the people of Congo and the people of Russian, when there is much terrible oppression and terrible atrocity committed in India, for example, killing two millions of people every year and outraging our women. In case, this country is occupied by Germans, and an Englishman not bearing to see the Germans walking with the insolence of conquerors in the streets of London, goes or kills one or two of Germans, then that Englishman is to be held as a patriot of the people of this country, then certainly I am a patriot too, working for the emancipation of my motherland. Whatever else I have to say is in my statement which is in the court.[27]

Dhingra concluded:

I made this statement not because I wish to plead for mercy or anything of that kind. I wish that English people should sentence me to death for in that case, the vengeance of my countrymen will be all the more keen. I put forward this statement to show the justice of my cause to the outside world especially to our sympathisers in America and Germany. That is all.

Dhingra had wanted to read aloud his last pronouncement before the magistrate which he was refused. He had referred to it in the course of his trial, but it was not made public. Savarkar never believed in missing opportunities, and was anxious that Dhingra's statement should receive the widest possible publicity because he thought that its publication would not only create a great impression but further the revolutionary cause. He contacted David Garnet who used his influence, and the statement appeared in the *Daily News* on 18 August 1909. And this was Garnet's account of the background:

I met Savarkar shortly afterwards and he gave me a copy of Dhingra's statement and asked me if I could get it published. That was easy. I took my first and only journalistic scoop to Robert Lynd and then on the staff of the *Daily News*, and it appeared in the paper next morning. Savarkar was extremely pleased.[28]

The Assassination

Dhingra's statment entitled "Challenge" is as follows:

I admit, the other day I attempted to shed English blood as an humble revenge for the inhuman hangings and deportations of patriotic Indian youths. In this attempt I have consulted none but my own conscience. I have conspired with none but my own duty.

I believe that a nation held down by foreign bayonet is in a perpetual state of war, since open battle is rendered impossible to disarmed race. I attacked by surprise; since guns were denied me I drew forth my pistol and fired.

As an Hindoo I felt that wrong to my country is an insult to my God. Her cause is the cause of Shri Ram, her service is the service of Shri Krishna. Poor in wealth and intellect, a son myself has nothing else to offer to the mother but his own blood, and so I have sacrificed the same on her altar.

The only lesson required in India at present is to learn how to die, and the only way to teach it is by dying ourselves. Therefore, I die, and glory in my martyrdom.

My only prayer of God is may I be reborn of the same mother and may I re-die in the same sacred cause till the cause is successful, and she stands free for the good humanity and to the glory of God—Bande Matram.[29]

Dhingra's trial was rather simple because there was no defence, no witness, and no argument. He admitted that he had killed Sir Curzon Wyllie, which he had intended to do. The whole thing was over in about an hour and a half. The Attorney General had urged the Chief Justice that the trial be "conducted without a word of political heroics, and treated as soberly as an ordinary murder."[30] It was proposed that Dhingra should be sent to Broadmoor for life, and that his execution might produce dangerous reprecussions in India, and threaten the lives of lonely British civilians serving in distant places among hostile elements, but the authorities decided otherwise, and sentenced him to death.

There was a great deal of hectic activity in India House two or three days preceding Dhingra's execution,[31] and men tended to appear more busy than actually they were. S.M. Master and Koregaonkar had made an application to the Deputy-Governor of Pentonville prison for permission to be present at the execution, but this was refused. However, Master was allowed to attend the inquest as a representative of the "Parsi" newspapers,[32] but his request for permission to see the prisoner was refused.

The 17th August was fixed for the execution of Dhingra, and he walked to the scaffold without assistance, and went to the gallows. I think that Bismal, the Urdu poet, had Dhingra in mind when he composed the following Urdu verse:

Sar firoshi ki tamana ab hamaray dil men hai,
Dekna hai zor kitna bazuay katal men hai.
(We are consumed with the passion to sell our head, we have to test the strength of the executing hand.)

Dwarkar Das, Savarkar, and Aiyer requested the Governor to be allowed to take away the body, but they were informed that the Governor was unable to see them, and to comply with their requests, and they expressed their disappointment, and left.[33] It is not clear from evidence whether Dhingra was buried or cremated. According to G.S. Khaparade who lived in London those days as a visitor, and who wrote his diary daily, Dhingra wanted his body to be cremated according to Hindu rites.[34] The question is why should the authorities not allow Dhingra's body to be cremated when he had asked for it. If they had not allowed the cremation, Savarkar and the young fire-brand revolutionaries would have created a furore over it, and made it another issue of public debate and criticism, particularly in the press and their writings, and the fact that they did not do so suggests that the authorities complied with Dhingra's request. Those youngmen were always bound to seize on British lapses and exploit them to their advantage for arousing national passions. But it seems that Savarkar and his followers were absorbed in larger issues like the impact of Dhingra's execution on the public mind. Again, if Dhingra had not been cremated, then Khaparade, who provides such details about Dhingra and his contemporaries, would have specifically mentioned that Dhingra's wishes had been thwarted. But the mere fact that Khaparade is absolutely silent on it shows that things took their normal course, and that Dhingra was cremated according to Hindu rites. It may be that Khaparade did not think it a big issue enough to merit his attention.

The note from the Criminal Intelligence office stated that Dhin-

The Assassination

gra's body would "most probably be cremated"[35] which mean sreally that they did not know what was really going to happen. In the *Civil and Military Gazette*, 19 August 1909, an entry figures that "Dhingra's request that his body might be cremated was refused."[36] So, the authorities had decided to bury Dhingra's body in accordance with the existing practice. The Government of India had requested the Home authorities: "We do not want the ashes of the martyr sent to India by parcel."[37] It was naturally feared that the ashes might receive a hero's welcome in India, and stir unrest, if not a widespread agitation, highly embarrassing, especially for the liberal-minded Lord Morley.

And then about Dhingra's end, Blunt wrote:

Some little time before the execution took place a large crowd gathered outside the approach of the prison, but it was noticeable that there were very few Indian students among those present. Shortly after nine o'clock the under-sheriff left the prison; in reply to the question how the execution passed off, said that everything had been in order and that "death had been instantaneous." Pierpoint was the executioner. An application for leave to have the body cremated was refused and it will be buried, in accordance with the usual custom, within the walls of the prison.[38]

4 Why Did Dhingra Shoot Wyllie?

The question arises why did Dhingra kill Sir Curzon Wyllie? The answer lies in knowing why should a raw young man brought up in a rich, influential and singularly loyal family to the British emerge into a revolutionary, involving himself in the murder of an individual who for one was closely connected with his family, and who had not in any way done any harm to him personally. One might ask why should an educated Indian young man studying in England kill an English official? Connected with these is the larger issue whether Dhingra's act was that of an individual, or part of a carefully planned conspiracy by the inmates of India House; and if it was a conspiracy then why should Dhingra have been singled out, and punished, and not others if they were involved in it. But if it was an individual act animated with some personal grievance or patriotic feelings then there seems no reason for seeking an explanation of his action in the activities of young revolutionaries in India House. It is clear from the nature of the evidence that the Home authorities were thorough and devious in their approach to the whole affair, and they seemed to paper over the real issues in the rush of things. Dhingra's action had really upset the apple cart.

After all, why should Dhingra have made Wyllie his target and why should he have killed him? Wyllie was not a policy-maker in the British hierarchy, he was a *persona-non-grata*, just an official of no great influence, a political Aide-e-camp to the Secretary of State for India, whose duties primarily were advising the Secretary of State on political questions relating to "native states" and making arrangements for the reception of Indians at courts. The killing of a heavy-weight was bound to create a bigger sensation, and make the assassin a hero in the eyes of his countrymen. The heavy-weight could be the Secretary of State for India, the Viceroy of India, the Governor of Province or a retired official from India who had acquired notoriety for perpetrating crimes on the

Why Did Dhingra Shoot Wyllie?

people of India. But Wyllie was none of these.

While this writer was engaged in studying and collecting material on Dhingra's motives, Dr S.K. Dutta, Vice-Chancellor, Kurukshetra University, mentioned in the course of discussions, that while in England in early thirties of this century, he had heard that Dhingra's real intention was to kill the Secretary of State for India. This view which tended to represent Wyllie's murder as a tragedy of mischance suggested a new line of enquiry. In the reconstruction of any historical event or personality, the most essential ingredient is evidence, the importance of which has often been undermined by such practitioners of history who are obsessed with the habit of general theorization. To clear up the mystery surrounding Dhingra's motive for action, it is necessary to see and use further contemporary evidence.

It became clear from the Intelligence reports of Scotland Yard which kept a close watch on the activities of the young revolutionaries including Dhingra that Dhingra had been hunting for the Secretary of State of India, Lord Morley, and the former Viceroy, Lord Curzon, for at least six months.[1] Lord Morley was then a key-figure in the realm of policy-making, and his scheme of liberal concessions to satisfy India's rising hopes was viewed by young revolutionaries like Dhingra as a subtle design to pacify Indian political leaders and thereby to quell any possibility of revolutionary activity in India. Lord Curzon was another target for revolutionaries because of the repressive policy which he had inaugurated with passionate zeal when he was the Viceroy of India. In his diary, 15 October 1908, Fredrick Arthur Histzel wrote: "Ever since May 1907, there were rumours of an Indian plot to assassinate J.M. [John Morley] which grew so alarming after October 1908 that he was secretly shadowed."[2] The same writer states that Lord Curzon was anxious enough about his own safety to put himself under police protection in those days.[3] But the reason why Dhingra could not kill either of them was that they were not accessible to him. On the contrary, Wyllie exposed himself to the public eye, and met Indian students quite often, and attended their functions, whenever he was invited to do so.

Would it mean then that Dhingra killed Wyllie simply because he was an Englishman associated with the British Raj? That would be an oversimplification. A man of Wyllie's calibre could not be ignored by the inmates of India House. He was arrogant, much too officious, and by his overbearing manners he had caused offence to Indian students. His past record had aroused hostile feelings; for example, how could Krishanvarma, the founder of India House, forget him? Wyllie had humiliated Krishnavarma when he was resident in Udaipur, and had disallowed him to be presented to the Viceroy; he had also prevented Krishnavarma from being employed in the service of the Udaipur Court. All these bitter memories rankled in his heart and he shared them with Savarkar and his other associates. It is unlikely that Dhingra was unaware of these unfortunate experiences which Krishanvarma had to suffer at the hands of Wyllie in India, and which must have greatly upset and infuriated Savarkar. Thus, to the inmates of India House including Dhingra, Wyllie came to be identified with that ruthless Imperial attitude of a ruling power which mars all future prospects of a promising young man, and throws him in a state of utter helplessness only because he has the ability to think for himself and to chalk out an independent programme of activities. So the young men at India House reacted sharply to Wyllie.

Besides this general feeling of suspicion which the inmates of India House shared towards Wyllie, the question arises what was Dhingra's attitude towards him. Dhingra had known Wyllie for a number of years in India, Wyllie had been a friend of the Dhingra family, and after his return to England, the Dhingra family carried on correspondence with him. When Kundan Lal, the eldest brother of Madan Lal, visited England, he met Wyllie. When reports reached the Dhingra family in India that Madan was staying in India House, and that he was closely associated with the political activities there, Kundan Lal wrote a letter to Sir Curzon Wyllie to look after the boy, and bring him round on the right path. Because of the obligations which Wyllie felt he had for the Dhingra family, he wrote the following letter,[4] on 13 April 1909, to Dhingra about two and a half months before he was shot:

Your brother Mr. Kundan Lal Dhingra, whose acquaintance I had the pleasure of making in England, has written to tell me that you are in London, and asking me to be of any assistance I can to you.

I expect to be abroad from the 15 to 30th April, but on my return I shall be very pleased to see you at the India House if

you can conveniently call between 11 and 1 or 2.30 and 3.30.
                               I remain
                           yours faithfully
                        WHC Wyllie, Lt. Col.

But Dhingra ignored this letter, and he did not meet Wyllie. He knew that Wyllie's aim was to dissuade him from identifying himself with the group of revolutionaries in India House; naturally he reacted violently to it because he thought that it was none of Wyllie's business to interfere in his private or public affairs. To a sensitive young man this type of patronizing gesture or instructive caution could be an affront. Wyllie replied to Kundan Lal saying that he had written and sent his message, but had received no reply, adding, of course, the explanation, "that it was not easy to get hold of youngmen at India House" which probably assuaged the family's anxiety. Emma Josephine Beck, Honorary Secretary, National Indian Association, whom Wyllie had asked for Dhingra's address, also wrote to Dhingra on 5 May 1909, requesting him to see Sir Curzon Wyllie.[5] Wyllie probably thought that he had better approach Dhingra through Miss Beck who because of her work at the National Indian Association enjoyed the reputation of a sympathetic and helpful person among Indian students. There is no evidence available to show Dhingra's reactions to this letter. But one cannot resist stating that Dhingra had begun to feel strongly that he was being shadowed by the authorities, and that some of the officials, who happened to be closely associated with his family in India, were adopting a patronizing attitude towards him which he was bound to resent, of course, like any sensitive, independent, self-respecting individual. Wyllie's letter to Kundan Lal must have disturbed the Dhingra family, and it was natural for them to write to Madan Lal. This caused greater resentment to Madan confirming his suspicion that things were being manipulated behind his back.

Madan Lal's father was known to be a strong-willed, despotic personality, and surely he could not tolerate his son's rude, erratic, and highly irresponsible behaviour. Wiser counsels, expostulations, and threats made no difference to Madan. He went his own way. He had gone rather too far, and could not possibly retreat. Could one then say that Dhingra killed Wyllie because Wyllie was meddling with his style of life, and shadowing over him on behalf of his family? To kill a person on that ground alone seems woefully out of proportion to the grievance one nurses. Perhaps, there is no logic in actions inspired by strong passions.

According to his family members, Madan Lal's act of shooting was the result of his unsoundness of mind which he had begun to show since his childhood, and of his eccentricity which grew gradually worse. Madan's erratic and odd behaviour formed the main subject of some of the letters which his family addressed to the Viceroy and other officials after Wyllie's assassination.[6] In these letters specific examples were cited to emphasize how at certain moments in life he had been swayed by wild passions resulting in violent action. By this plea for the unsoundness of his mind, the family tried to put a charitable construction on his action, and cover up his guilt. The idea behind this type of defence was to save him, at least, from the gallows if not to exonerate him completely. In the light of this plea, Dhingra's act was not politically motivated, but impulsive and irrational which deserved, on merits, a benefit of doubt. In order to determine the veracity of the family's contention that Madan was of unsound mind, it is necessary to look closely into the examples of his odd behaviour cited.

According to his family, some of the examples of Madan's curious behaviour were as follows: his running away from home in early life, and his joining as a *laskar*[7] for about six months; his habit of teasing children, and subjecting them to irritating experiences; his melancholic temperament of brooding over things; and his disinclination to stick to one job. His brothers pointed out to the Private Secretary to the Viceroy, another incident exemplifying Madan's erratic behaviour in England: they wrote that one day Madan cut off the whiskers of a pet cat of the landlady in his lodgings, and when his elder brother Kundan Lal remonstrated with him, he was furious, and left the lodgings quietly, and shifted elsewhere. He never wrote from England to his family unless he wanted money which he always preferred to receive from Thomas Cook and Sons; not even in one of his letters did he ever express feelings of love or affection for any one of his relations—his letters were always formal, businesslike, too short, and almost like items in a telephone directory. Madan's brothers showed one of these letters to Dunlop Smith, Private Secretary to the Viceroy, who wrote to the Secretary of State: "They [Madan's brothers] showed me one letter to his father asking for a remittance, which is certainly a most unbusinesslike and almost unintelligible document."⁸

In the early months of 1909 Madan avoided even meeting his younger brother Bhajan Lal whom he had admonished earlier for interfering with his life.

The above-mentioned examples do not by any means show the unsoundness of Madan's mind, but at most they do reflect a waywardness, traits of eccentricity, and an explosive temper—the habits of mind of a sensitive and repressed individual who is out of tune with his environment. He was a whimsical sort of fellow, somewhat impulsive, and highly strung. The plea of his unsoundness of mind was strictly a design on the part of his family to save him from the gallows, and it was their last flickering hope. If he had an unsound mind then the question arises how could his family send him abroad for higher studies, and bear such an enormous expense? Surely, a person of an unsound mind could not undertake higher studies in engineering. There is no evidence that for his mental disability he was ever treated in England; otherwise his family would have mentioned this fact along with the name of the doctor who attended on him.

The Dhingra family without losing any time had acted swiftly, and on 5 July 1909, only four days after Wyllie's murder, sent a cable to Bhajan Lal Dhingra, in London, "Refer Mental unsoundness from childhood. Express Abhorrence, through solicitor."⁹ The Home Government did take into consideration this plea of the unsoundness of mind, and referred this matter to the Medical Officer of Brixton Prison who attended on Dhingra for about a month and a half, and found him absolutely normal, and repudiated completely the view of his mental instability. In his report, Dyer, the Medical Officer, said:

> He [Dhingra] is well-educated, of an intellectual type, somewhat reticent in conversation and retiring in manner. He eats and sleeps well; converses quite rationally and sensibly on all topics; has behaved in a quiet and sane manner, and shown no sign of insanity.¹⁰

The medical report dismisses the plea of the unsoundness of Dhingra's mind. Blunt in his diary wrote:

> It was recorded in the medical evidence at the trial that when

arrested, Dhingra's pulse beat no quicker than was normal nor from first to last has he shown any sign of weakening.[11]

But the Dhingra family, namely, his father and brothers, persisted in their letters on his insanity; and the Secretary of State in his cable of 14 August 1909 settled the whole matter when he asked the Viceroy:

> Please inform relations of Dhingra that after considering all circumstances including evidence of father and brother, Home Secretary regrets he cannot advise his Majesty to interfere with the due course of the law.[12]

Dhingra's landlady, Mary Harris, with whom Madan resided at 108 Ledbury Road, said in the court that he was a steady youngman, very regular in habits, who stayed mostly at home after 7 o'clock.[13] She found no reasons to complain about his behaviour. Similarly Emma Joseph Beck, Honorary Secretary, National Indian Association, whom he used to meet at functions, mentioned no abnormal trait in his behaviour.[14] According to his teachers, Karl Pearson and J.D. Carnac of University College,[15] his academic progress was satisfactory; he was diligent in his studies, fairly regular in his classes, was a mediocre student, and his chief interests were drawing (graphs) and mechanical engineering.

From the evidence of Dhingra's acquaintances who knew him well enough, and the Medical Officer under whose care he spent his days in the prison, it is clear that Madan was a normal person, in full possession of his faculties. Therefore, by no stretch of imagination could Dhingra be labelled as insane.

Dhingra's act was neither a venture of unsound mind nor a freak of chance, but a wilful murder. To say that he killed Wyllie because he nursed a personal grievance against him would be a facile generalization, though it must be recognized that Wyllie's insolence in throwing his weight around had annoyed Dhingra who felt slighted by Wyllie's meddlesome interest in his doings: he believed that Wyllie was inquiring impertinently into his movements and associations. These personal factors, vital but not decisive, in the complexity of the motives of his action cannot be ignored. Wyllie had become quite an unpopular figure among the Indian community because of his arrogance and the perverse influence that he was supposed to wield on the Indian office, and he provoked thus strong criticism among the Indian revolutionaries, but this does not mean that there was an agreed plan to kill him. By no means could it be said that the youngmen of India House regarded him as the chief villian. Behind Dhingra's motives for Wyllie's murder, there lay his complete and total commitment to Savarkar and, to his ideology of militant nationalism, besides of course, his personal dislike of Wyllie for the reasons mentioned earlier.

Savarkar had cast a spell over the young men at India House and, Dhingra like others, had thrown in his lot with him. Savarkar has particularly mentioned in his recollections *Six Glorious Epochs of Indian History*, where he surveyed the programme and ideals of revolutionary movement, that Dhingra was "converted to our revolutionary views through my principles and guidance."[16] One of the chief means that Savarkar adopted to ensure commitment of his followers to the cause of the liberation of India was to administer to them an oath of complete loyalty to his revolutionary programme. The loyalty meant absolute surrender and obedience to him in whatever he was to plan.

Savarkar has specifically highlighted some of the names of his followers to whom he administered the oath in secrecy. While recollecting the character of his revolutionary activity, he wrote:

> To the thousands of members of my revolutionary secret society, the Abhinav Bharat Samastha, right from its original nucleus at Nasik and Bhagur to its numerous branches in many foreign countries I had myself administered the oath of allegiance in person. The martyrs were Madan Lal Dhingra, Lala Hardyal, Bhai Parmanand, Chatterjee, Senapati Bapat, Dr. Jayaswal, Rishi, Arya—many names can one recount.[17]

Of his close followers, Savarkar put the name of Dhingra on the top which is a recognition of the most outstanding service that he rendered for the fulfilment of Savarkar's ideals. The sphere in which Savarkar manifested his ingenuity was psychology. He knew men's vices and desires, he knew their hidden ambitions, he knew where they were gullible, where they were strong, and where they were weak. The intensity of his faith in the liberation of his country, and the novelty of his revolutionary programme had a tremendous appeal to his followers.

Savarkar could give his whole heart to men who were willing to be martyred for the faith. Dhingra was his staunch follower, and was fascinated by Savarkar's magneticism. He had found also in Savarkar a guide and a mentor, someone to look up to, filling a vacuum when he was being alienated from his family. His parents' high standard of obedience and achievement had been in some instances a burden than an inspiration; he had chafed under the restraints of life, and at times he was seized with a sense of vertigo from which he could never recover. On the other hand, Savarkar found in Dhingra, a well-dressed, handsome young lad, coming from a rich family, somewhat obstinate, of uneasy mind, needing a release of his pent-up feelings, a reliable instrument to execute his plans. Both needed each other; Dhingra needed Savarkar for his psychological satisfaction, and Savarkar needed Dhingra for his political ends. So their close relationship was determined by psychological and political objects. "Ifs" in history are dangerous, but their use in historical investigation tends to clarify issues which otherwise remain obscure. If Dhingra had not come in contact with Savarkar, it is difficult to know what would have been his interests and line of activities, but his close attachment to Savarkar and to his ideology determined for him the entire course of the life he was to follow. Savarkar was the guiding spirit, and the architect of the revolutionary movement in England which had gained considerable impetus, and which was becoming a subject of severe criticism by some of the Indian political leaders like B.C. Pal and Gokhale because of its stark radicalism and open propagation of violence. By the use of his marvellous oratorical skills, and remarkable organizational ability, he created that climate of opinion which provided incentive and encouragement to Dhingra and others to plunge into the revolutionary movement. Dhingra came to be what he was mainly due to Savarkar who moulded his life.

Savarkar would not leave anything to chance. He believed firmly that for any revolutionary activity, training in the use of arms was absolutely necessary. He initiated Dhingra and his other followers in taking lessons in shooting for which he made arrangements with Henry Stanton Morley at Tottenham Court Road. After Dhingra's arrest, the police headed by Alfred Draper, Detective Inspector, recovered the following items from his lodgings 108, Ledbury Road: 63 loose cartridges; a magazine containing seven cartridges; a gun licence issued to him on 26 January 1909; a record book showing the results of pistol practices dated 15 and 29 May; and five cartridge cases.[18] Dhingra had been learning how to shoot from early 1909, and continued practising on the range at Tottenham Road right until the day when he killed Wyllie.[19] In fact, he was quite regular in May and June, and though there was no fixed time for him to go to the range, sometime he would reach there about 12 or 1 P.M. or in the evening about 5 as it suited him. He had purchased the pistol, the Colt Automatic Magazine from Messers Gamage Limited, Holborn on 26 January, and started going to the range the same day. Henry Stanton Morley who taught Dhingra at the range has given a vivid account of his shooting practice. According to him, Dhingra practised with his own pistol and ammunition, and attended the range for about two to three months. He spoke to hardly anyone and concentrated on his work. Morley said in Court:

> He [Dhingra] used to have 10 shots at a time and pay 6d. He used to take deliberate aim and pause between each shot and sometime they were fired more rapidly together. I think he improved slightly in his shooting. Targets of paper were provided by me. He used a Colts' automatic pistol; it ejects the spent cartridge immediately it has been fired, and automatically another cartridge from the magazine covers up in its place. Dhingra used automatic pistol—no one else then. Prisoner's cartridges were smokeless.[20]

Dhingra took his shooting practice rather seriously. By no means was he a fine shot; he had acquired some proficiency in it, and could just manage to do his job fairly well. But he kept his shooting practice a dead secret. Even his landlady did not know of it. When she was asked whether she ever saw any weapons in his lodgings, she stoutly denied it. It means that Dhingra had hid them carefully; even his brother who was in London knew nothing of these shooting practices.

It might be interesting to see how Dhingra spent the day on 1 July 1909 when he killed Wyllie because the way he passed that day, his activities, and the individuals he met with, may offer a clue to the whole plan of murder. He did not meet Savarkar on 1 July as he was not in London; he had left for Reading a day or two before. This absence of Savarkar from the scene of the grim tragedy was deliberate. Dhingra's landlady, Mary Harris, said that he had spent most of his time in his lodgings, and "did not go much in the evening."[21] When cross-examined, she stated that he had left his lodgings about 2 P.M. or a little before dinner, and returned home about 6 P.M. or a little before. Thus Dhingra remained out almost for five hours, and it was in that period that he went in for his usual shooting practice.

According to his shooting coach, Morley, Dhingra was at the range on 1 July at about 5.30 P.M. On 28 June he had visited the range at 12 noon, and fired twelve shots, on 1 July, Morley saw Dhingra again fire twelve shots at a target from a very close range. Dhingra asked Morley to clear his pistol which he did by rubbing the pouch through the barrel. In his evidence, Morley confirmed with regard to the pistol that "it was the similar weapon to the one he always used." He remembered vividly Dhingra's performance at the range, and found nothing unusual or peculiar in his behaviour. At the end of his evidence in the Court, Morley said softly, "that after cleaning his pistol," gave it to him. He then left the place and he was never to return to the range again.

After the shooting practice Dhingra returned to his lodgings at about 6.30 P.M. He left his lodgings again 7 or 8 P.M. He was going to attend the function at the National Indian Association in the Imperial Institute. He was dressed in an English dark lounge suit, and wore a blue turban. He went out in a cab. It is clear from the evidence available that he did not go straight to the Imperial Institute. On the contrary, he went to see some of his associates near his lodgings, in a restaurant, the Indian Catering Company which was managed by Nizam-ud-Din. The Intelligence Report states that Dhingra was "alleged to have been plied with *bhang*, before setting out to commit the outrage."[22]

The taking of *bhang* before Wyllie's murder was intentional because *bhang* relieves the tensions and conflicts to which the human mind is susceptible, particularly in crucial matters, weakens the hold of rationality, almost destroys, though temporarily, the sense to discriminate between good and evil, and creates that state of mind when rational instincts are overpowered by passions of indifference, when "theirs not to reason why, theirs but to do or die." From the eye-witness account of people like Charles Rolleston, Emma Josephine Beck, and Dr Buchanan who saw Dhingra after Wyllie's murder, it is evident that he was absolutely calm, and was "the calmest of persons in the crowd."[23] This extraordinary calmness of mind might have been a result of the use of *bhang* and, from this point of view, there seems nothing reprehensible in it. But it might be argued that calmness of mind was perhaps natural after the murder. What else could Dhingra do? He could not be an agitated person after an event of such tragic magnitude, particularly when he was surrounded by a large crowd gazing on him with baleful and annihilating glare. But there seems little reason to disregard the Intelligence report which states that "Dhingra took *bhang*." In his evidence Charles Rolleston said that Dhingra had "a half dazed dreamy manner which made me suspect he might have taken bhang."[24] Dhingra took *bhang* as a part of the plan, to leave nothing to chance, and to expel even the remotest possibility of running away from the duty of killing an Englishman.

On the evening of Wyllie's murder, Dhingra visited some of his friends. According to the information received from Scotland Yard, he accompanied a "pock-marked man" (later identified as Dr T.S.S. Rajan) to H.K. Koregaonkar's lodgings.[25] Dhingra arrived in the Imperial Institute for the National Indian Association function at about 9 P.M. Emma Joseph Beck, Hon. Secretary, National Indian Association, who knew Dhingra well and, who had corresponded with him previously, talked to him for about half an hour.[26] She found in him nothing unusual, and he appeared absolutely normal in his behaviour. When she enquired about his future plans, he replied that he intended to take up A.M.I.C.E. examination in October, after which he proposed returning to India. As often happens at such social functions, Dhingra mixed leisurely among his friends and acquaintances. Nobody noticed anything peculiar in him, and nobody could suspect that something dreadful would happen for which he would take the initiative. Some of Dhingra's close friends were there, but not Savarkar who had preferred to keep himself away, and people were in a light mood exchanging pleasantries.

One might conjecture what was Dhingra up to, and what were his thoughts. For one thing, he was carrying arms in his pockets to finish the task assigned, and for another, he was sorely disappointed because none of the heavy-weights was there whom he would have preferred to kill. Neither Morley nor Curzon could be expected in a function of the National Indian Association, though Dhingra kept hoping for them to arrive. Sir Charles Lyall and Lady Lyall were there, but Sir Charles had the reputation of a soft well-meaning innocuous sort of person who was somewhat mild towards Indians. At the function, light snacks and tea were served, and some musical items presented. All this must have strained Dhingra's tense nerves and, possibly, he could not enjoy that evening the charms and delights of lively female company and conversation, his mind was elsewhere, his thoughts wandered, but probably the mild effect of intoxication had a soothing effect on him, though it had warmed his blood, and as usual, he was polite, courteous, and impeccable in manners. But he seemed basically disappointed for he was not sure who to pick, and who to kill; disappointed because there was neither a Morley, Curzon, nor any other high official who had acted as a red rag to the Indian bull.

Sir Curzon Wyllie entered the Jehangir Hall about 9.30 P.M., almost half an hour after Dhingra's arrival.[27] According to Scotland Yard, Koregaonkar was also present in the hall, and he had been sent by Savarkar to make sure that Dhingra did not flinch from the assigned task—Rajan and Dhingra had earlier visited Koregaonkar at his residence.[28] When Wyllie entered the hall, Koregaonkar is reported to have told Dhingra, "Look out." Dhingra had come prepared to kill a British heavy-weight but was naturally disconcerted in not finding him there. In this despondent state, his eyes fell on Wyllie who had incurred the Indian student community's wrath because of his sinister design of shadowing their movements. Dhingra had also felt humiliated at his hands— Wyllie had been meddling with his private affairs on behalf of his family. It seems that in the hall he was still vacillating—maybe, due to intoxication, irresolution, or diminishing hopes of finding Morley or Curzon. He wanted to strike off the heads of the tall poppies, but they were not to be found there. After a delightful evening, people were streaming out, and Wyllie too was leaving the hall when Koregaonkar said to Dhingra, "*Aji Jao na, Kya Karte ho*" (Well, go on, what are you doing?).[29] Dhingra moved up, engaged Wyllie in conversation as he was coming out of the door in the vestibule, fired four shoots from close range of three or four feet, and Wyllie fell dead.

On 4 July three days after Wyllie's murder, a meeting of the young Indian revolutionaries took place in India House, and about twelve of them were present. The proceedings of this meeting have been reported by Scotland Yard through one of its agents who was present at the meeting. This report is valuable because of the eye-witness account it gives, and also because it confirms that behind the whole plan of murder lay Savarkar's inspiration and guidance.[30] Savarkar had master-minded the whole thing. Dhingra had completely surrendered himself to Savarkar's ideology and programme. This is the stuff of which revolutionaries are made: the one to plan, and the other to obey. True revolutionaries are not much given to talking; they merely act, and their commitments are shrouded in mystery. This special type of relationship between a leader and a follower is moulded by political commitments, and psychological tensions. It would be an incomplete story of the revolutionaries to say that they are motivated only by political ideas and beliefs; to say this is to see only the tip of the ice-berg. Such a naive version purges history of the intangible ephemera of the habits, attitudes, experiences, and moral stance that gives them particular character.

At the meeting in India House on 4 July there was great deal of excitement. Aiyer paid an eloquent tribute to Dhingra's act which he described as "glorious" and said: "There was some one among them who was the real *guru*, the *Avatar* of Krishna who had produced a man like Dhingra."[31] He hinted later on that it was V.D. Savarkar (he did not then name him) who had "thought and prepared Dhingra to do all he did."[32] Savarkar too spoke briefly on this occasion, and said, "There was one man to watch and guide the whole thing" and added that "Dhingra stood cool and calm, firing at the prostrate figure of his country's enemy, Wyllie."[33] Here Savarkar admitted the decisive role he played in the grim drama. Every Englishman was India's enemy—that was then Savarkar's political philosophy. Dr Rajan, whom Dhingra had accompanied to Koregaonkar on 1 July, said in the course of conversation that "Dhingra was the product of Savarkar's sound teaching."[34] Dr Rajan also added that Dhingra had also been hunting for Lord Morley and Lord Curzon for the last seven months, but he could not lay his hands on either of them. The Scotland Yard report concluded that it would therefore appear that the murder was engineered by Savarkar with the assistance of Aiyer, Rajan and Koregaonkar."[35] Savarkar would never like the fight to end with Wyllie's murder; the fight must be intensified and continued. He warned: "It is an initial step: I have still to avenge my brother's life."[36] This referred to his brother Ganesh who had been transported for life on 9 June 1909 at Nasik.

It would be clear from the above account that Dhingra was committed to Savarkar and to his ideology for which his motives were mixed. These motives were both political and psychological, and it is rather difficult to say which of them were primary. The traumatic experience of humiliations, bitterness, and frustration creates a weird world of its own, and leads sensitive and intelligent men to introspection, and search for identity. These men are swayed by passions, and they pour forth their loves, their hates, and their blind urges in the form of revenge. They resort to settling their accounts, and dealing blows to those who dare to humble them. In this case of Wyllie's murder, the account had to be settled; the account of personal humiliations was transposed into the humiliation of the millions of his countrymen, and this transposition and projection is inevitable where tenacity of will, idealism, and intelligence are in full play. This is not to suggest that Savarkar and Dhingra were not inspired by the pure and noble flame of patriotism. Patriotic they were; but there is more to it than meets the eye. Patriotism is a complex thing, and so many strands give it a form; an intense passionate love for one's country is the essential ingredient of patriotism but this passion sometimes originates in a curious manner; behind it may be a whole world of experience of frustrations, disillusionments, ambitions, morbid reactions, and many hidden complexes which are churned over by inner drives to take the form of concrete ideas and ideologies.

This writer emphasizes a strong need for the study of revolutionaries from a psychological point of view;[37] to study them from the ideological angle would not explain the complexity of their motives, nor would economic factors unravel the deeper inner urges which sting men into action. The entire world of emotions and passions has to be laid bare. In the case of Savarkar and Dhingra, Wyllie's murder was an act of revenge for the grievous wrongs that they suffered at the hands of certain individuals which influenced and moulded their attitudes, and became the bedrock on which they set up their political beliefs and ideology, and their revolutionary activities.

5 The Impact

Dhingra's murder of Wyllie created a widespread sensation in official and political circles both in England and India. Lady Morley broke the tragic news to her husband on the early morning of 2 July, and he made no comment, and left immediately for the India Office. Naturally, Morley was shocked to lose in such tragic circumstances his political Aide-de-camp whose expert advice he had greatly valued on political matters. A week later he wrote to Sir Sydenham Clarke in India:

> I do not know if you were acquainted with poor Wyllie. A more kind, genial, unselfish and helpful creature never existed; nor could a more blind and purposeless piece of bloodshed, be imagined.[1]

Sir Lawrence Jenkins shared similar sentiments with Morley:

> Why he [Wyllie] of all men with his large store of kind sympathy for all things by an Indian should have been singled out for the tragic end. I cannot conceive: there is cruel irony in it all. And poor India: she, too, I suppose, must pay the penalty for this wicked madness; how poorly is she justified of her children.[2]

Morley and his colleagues saw in Wyllie's assassination not only a tragic episode which had cost a precious life, but a symptom of things portentous fraught with dangerous consequences on a wide scale. If the Secretary of States' political Aide-de-camp, a high official in the British hierarchy, could end up like this, then surely many British officers in India were exposed to grave danger who were serving out in far-off, isolated places. It seemed as though worse things lay in store for the British.

The news of Wyllie's murder reached India by Reuters. The

Intelligence Department of the Government of India suspected that the assassin was a Bengali,³ but this suspicion was removed when Dhingra admitted that he had killed Wyllie. In the first decade of the twentieth century, the British Government regarded Bengal as the nursery of revolutionaries, and whenever any political murder occurred, their eyes fell first on Bengal; but in the case of Wyllie's murder their conjecture proved wrong because the assassin was a Punjabi belonging to a rich family loyal to the British. Morley and his colleagues were determined to find out the truth about the criminal act, and to deter others from indulging in such nefarious activities in future. On 2 July 1909, Morley sent the following telegram to the Viceroy, Lord Minto:

> A most important thing to ascertain is whether the crime was the result of individual action or criminal conspiracy.⁴

Morley was convinced that the crime was politically motivated, and in his telegram to the Viceroy, he mentioned the "evil influence" that had worked on Dhingra in India House. Morley added:

> The brother of the murderer is K.L. Dhingra who writing from Amritsar March 24 begged Wyllie when he had met in England to get his brother away from the evil influence at India House. Sir Wyllie wrote but never received a reply from the man.⁵

Morley asked the Viceroy to "keep close watch on all the telegrams from Europe, especially by London, and Paris." He had reasons to believe that behind Dhingra's act there lay a wide network of conspiracy in which Dhingra had acted merely as an instrument. The Government of India informed the Director-General, Telegrams, about Morley's instructions; and even those telegrams in cipher or in language were scrutinized which on the face of it did not relate to the assassination.⁶ But these measures hardly gave any new information on the crime.

Madan's act was a terrible blow to his family which was both shocked and highly embarrassed. They had been deeply concerned for some time past about Madan's political activities in London, and had sought Sir Curzon's help to save him from the sinister influence of India House; they had also tried to bring him round

The Impact

through Kundan Lal, who had visited England, and Bhajan Lal, who was studying in London, but in vain. Polite letters from India crammed with requests and expostulations made no difference to Madan—he went his own way, and bothered not the least about these mediations. His entire attitude to the family, particularly from January 1909, was absolutely abnormal.[7] The family realized that Madan had gone astray, and would not listen to any advice, but they could hardly imagine that he would go to the length of killing an Englishman and, more so, a family friend like Wyllie, whose help they had sought to set Madan right. The family felt disgraced, and they bitterly repeated in their letters to the government that Madan had completely ruined the family prestige by his mad act. The Dhingra family looked at the whole episode from two different angles; for one thing, they believed that Madan would have to face the gallows, and for another, that the British would cease to repose any further confidence in them. Sir Curzon was their family friend and Madan's killing him, so they thought, was the basest example of ingratitude.

Thus the Dhingra family took the immediate step of expressing their abhorrence at the act. Their fairly large number of letters[8] to the British officials show how they suffered under the strain of mental torture. They found themselves utterly helpless, but still sought some ways to salvage their completely discredited position. In their letters they condemned Madan's act, lamented over their family friend Wyllie's death, and professed absolute loyalty to the British. They pleaded further with the government that Madan who had shown signs of eccentricity since his childhood deserved compassion due to his mental instability, a benefit, usually given to the handicapped, who are not in possession of their faculties.

On 5 July 1909 the family sent to Bhajan Lal, Madan's younger brother, in London, the following telegram:

Refer Mental unsoundness from childhood Express Family Abhorrence, Through Solicitor.[9]

In another telegram to the Private Secretary to the Viceroy, dated 4 July, Behari Lal Dhingra, Madan's elder brother, condemned Madan's act emphasizing his peculiar habits.

He added:

Though every man is responsible for his actions and must suffer himself, our whole family is filled with deepest shame and sorrow at Madan's act. He showed eccentricity in childhood and became generally worse.[10]

Behari Lal then singled out specific instances of Madan's odd behaviour, and concluded: "Gods will be done. Pray lay this before His Excellency."

Madan's murder of Wyllie was a severe blow to his father, Rai Sahib Ditta Mal, an old man, whom disgrace continued to haunt. Sahib Ditta's bitter agony is evident from the following poignant letter addressed to Dunlop Smith, Private Secretary to the Viceroy, dated 4 July:

You can imagine the shock I have sustained at this age on reading the news that my son has been the murderer of our esteemed friend, Col. Sir Curzon Wyllie. The whole family expresses its deep abhorrence of the horrible deed of this mad son of mine. He had no doubt shown signs of unsoundness of mind for the past ten years but I never expected that the cursed India House will prove so much an exciting cause, and that will kill a man who was a friend and a well-wisher and I have myself been trying as you might have already noticed ever since I came to know of his residence at the India House, to dissuade my son from such evil company as that of Krishnavarma and the India House and been asking Sir Wyllie to use his influence with my son to make him desist from such company.

I assure you I am not so much sorry to lose my son as I am for his killing two innocent men and proving a disgrace to his family which had always been so loyal and grateful to the Government for its numerous favours. I am not quite about myself at present and cannot write more.[11]

Most of the letters addressed by the family to the authorities were repetitive: condemnation of Wyllie's murder, Madan's unsoundness of mind from his childhood, and the family's loyalty to the government. The family made persistent efforts to impress upon the authorities their strong disapproval of Madan's act, which had humiliated them in the public eye; they assured the government that they would never regard Madan as a martyr, but a lunatic

tic who had allowed himself to be used as an instrument by perverse elements beyond their control; and they urged the authorities to track down the whole conspiracy in which Madan played a subsidiary part. They further pleaded with the government to take a lenient view of Madan's act in view of his congenital mental abnormality.

Sahib Ditta directed his sons, Behari Lal and Mohan Lal, to meet Dunlop Smith, Private Secretary to the Viceroy, and their family friend, and express their disapproval of Madan's murder of Sir Curzon Wyllie. They met Dunlop Smith in Simla, and conveyed to him the entire family's great anguish over the tragic episode. When they were giving their version of the whole story, they broke down in sorrow, and the interview deeply moved Dunlop Smith, which he recorded in his diary as "very painful." They informed Dunlop Smith that Madan was an eccentric youth who had always treated his parents in a cavalier fashion; they emphasized that "he had not acted by himself, and was a tool because of his curious character"; and "they begged the whole matter to be sifted, thoroughly, because the outrage was the result of a conspiracy." Dunlop Smith listened to them patiently, and promised to discuss the matter with the Viceroy. The had approached the highest official authority in India with the request to take a compassionate view of Madan's awry act. All these steps were taken by the family without Madan's knowledge.

After this interview with Dunlop Smith, Mohan Lal and Behari Lal addressed a letter to him on 7 July describing mainly the history of Madan's mental abberations,[12] a cause of much anxiety and embarrassment all these years to the parents who had borne it with patience. This letter was written probably at the instance of Dunlop Smith when they wanted to convey their feelings on Madan's act to the Viceroy for his sympathetic consideration. As an experienced official, Dunlop Smith knew that verbal repentence, apologies or explanations would not carry any weight with the government on a matter of such serious import; something tangible was needed to strengthen his hand; hence this letter which did not add anything new on Madan's action, but recounted in detail some of the oddities in his behaviour since his childhood. This is the longest and most valuable of documents, produced by the Dhingra family, which throws light on the family's psychological tension and Madan's earlier career; it reflects the family's state of mind under the strain of tragedy; and there are embodied in it feelings of remorse, gratitude, sorrow, sympathy, and bitterness all rolled in one. Madan's brothers make it clear in their letter that they "have been deputed by our father who is too distressed to give his family's feelings."

It is not necessary to reproduce the whole letter here but to quote from it only such portions to which the family attached special importance. It is made clear at the outset that Madan's mad act had plunged the whole family into grief. "It is an irony of fate that in a family life like ours so deeply loyal to government and so gratefully attached to the British people, a youngman should degenerate himself into a murder."[13]

This letter reiterates how previously the family had stood by the British; for example, how their brother Chaman Lal Dhingra, Bar-at-law, during the Muzzafarpur Bomb case, had published an article in the *Civil and Military Gazette*, much to the annoyance of his countrymen, condemning the outrage and supporting the British policy. In this letter further assurance of loyalty is given to the government: "We are the foremost supporters of the Government and sincere admirers of the British nation."[14]

Further, an earnest request is made to the authorities to find out the whole truth about the tragedy because a strong feeling prevailed in the family that Madan had merely acted as an instrument in the hands of others. In the following extract Madan's responsibility for the assassination is played down:

> We want to know what exactly the causes of Madan's degeneration into a murderer have been as he was eccentric subject to fits of rashness; he was discovered as an excellent tool for evil purpose by Krishna Varma and his lieutenants. We think the statement that he was given bhang before the crime is likely to be correct.[15]

The letter then provides details about Madan's abnormality of mind, and specific cases of his peculiar behaviour, it gives instances how the family tried its best to mend his ways but in vain, and finally it lashes out severely at his associates who brought him misfortune, and his family a foul name. About their role and how cleverly they managed to escape, the letter states:

> ...the real culprits have kept themselves in the background.

They have succeeded in utilising a member of a loyal family for their evil purpose and they have wrecked three lives: Sir Curzon Wyllie, Dr. Lalcaca and ours.[16]

And finally the letter ends with an eloquent, and most effective condemnation of Madan's action, but also with a strong plea that he was a lunatic who had been exploited for their ends by crafty and wild machinations of others:

We shall not consider Madan Lal as a martyr, as the extremists would desire, we look upon him as a lunatic [who could not be influenced by the tradition and instincts of the family] and his act as a detestible role. May God punish the real culprits, and throw light so that everybody may be judged correctly.[17]

From this letter certain basic issues emerge which show the impact of tragedy on the Dhingra family; firstly, its sense of shame and horor at Wyllie's murder; secondly, its profession of loyalty to the British; thirdly, its denunciation of Madan's act; fourthly, its emphasis on Madan's abnormality of mind; and finally, its plea that Madan did not act independently on his own, but had been used by others.

Mohan Lal and Behari Lal wrote another letter to the Lieutenant Governor, Punjab, Sir Louis Dane, giving a detailed account of Madan's abnormality of mind; they emphasized also the peculiar and highly embarrassing situation to which they had been put due to their brother's shameful action. Sir Louis Dane tried to assuage their sorrow by the assurance that the government would not hold them responsible for Madan's act. Dane wrote:

I am much obliged to you for your full account of your unfortunate brother's career, and with your permission I propose to make this public. Before I knew who the murderer of Sir W. Curzon Wyllie and Dr. Lalkaka was, I had already stated how grievous was the disgrace to the Province that he was a Punjabi. The disgrace is notably deepened by the fact that he is a member of a family so well known and respected throughout the province, and one which has been fortunate in winning its way into the high favour of its fellow-citizens, of the ruling princes of India and of the British Government. Nothing that I can say will remove the deep sense of grief and shame under which you now labour but you may rest assured that neither Great Britain nor India, nor the people, nor Government, will ascribe any fault to your family for the rash act of a young man whose unhappy lot it has been to fall into the hands of those enemies of the human race in general, and of India in particular whose aim and object, it seems to be to render all sympathy and cordial cooperation in this country impossible; but, who have, I trust, in this case overreached themselves. I believe that the consequences of their crime will not only recoil upon their own heads, but will tend to promote that closer union of hearts in India which it was their wish to destroy. If this is the result, it should be in itself a solace to you. Assuring you of my fullest sympathy with your father and yourselves.[18]

It is clear from the correspondence of the Dhingra family which has been partly reproduced here that after the shock of the tragedy had somewhat subsided, the real worry of the family was to save Madan from the gallows, not in any way by rousing the British ire but by appealing to their goodwill. On the one hand, the family professed loyalty to the British, but on the other, it emphasized Madan's abnormality of mind. Could one say that by attempting to save Madan from the gallows, the family was justifying his action? Not the least. There is no contradiction in these two attitudes. The family condemned his action but did not want him to lose his life which is quite a normal attitude for a family to adopt placed in such circumstances. Due to the efforts of the family both through correspondence, and personal interviews with men in authority, the government considered the family plea of taking a compassionate view on Madan's action, but they were not willing to relent in any way. Madan was not repentant in any way; he stuck to his convictions, and justified his action. On 14 August 1909 three days before Madan's life was executed, the Secretary of State for India, wrote to the Viceroy:

Please inform relations of Dhingra that after considering all circumstances including evidence of father and brother, Home Secretary requests he cannot advise His Majesty to interfere with the due cause of the law.[19]

Madan's act of killing Wyllie was strongly criticized in Indian political circles. A meeting of Indian residents in London was held on 3 July, denouncing Dhingra's crime. Among those who spoke on the occasion included Surendra Nath Banerjee, Bipin Chandra Pal, J.M. Parikh, and G.S. Khaparde. In his diary, Khaparade who went to London to plead the case of Tilak wrote about the meeting as follows:

> Then I, Parikh, Pal and Phelps went to a vegetarian restaurant, had something to eat, and proceeded to the new Reform Club. The meeting was held in the smoking room and it was cram full. Surendra Babu presided and made a good speech but Bipin Babu's speech was the best of all. Some young man also spoke and I spoke on the resolutions. Mr. and Mrs. Dube were there. The former seconded the resolution thanking the chair. The meeting passed off very well. Its main object was to express abhorrence at the yesterday's crime and to declare that it had no connection with the agitation going on in India for political advancement.[20]

A big meeting of Indian residents in London took place in Caxton Hall on 5 July at 5.30 P.M. which was also attended by quite a number of Europeans. This meeting was arranged in order to "express the indignation of the Indian community in London at the murders." The Aga Khan who treated England as Islam's best friend presided.[21] Theodore Morrison conducted to the platform Madan Lal Dhingra's younger brother Bhajan Lal who was studying in England. Morrison said that Bhajan Lal had come there to "show before his fellow country men that he disassociated himself from the murderer."[22] Bhajan Lal was so overcome by emotions that he could hardly speak, and was led back to his place in the hall. Thereafter, the Agha Khan read out the resolutions in a faltering voice, looking utterly nervous:

> (1) That the General meeting, consisting of the representatives of all the communities of India and of the bulk of Indian residents in Great Britain express their horror and indignation with which they in common with the whole people of India view the dastardly crime committed by an obscure and ill-conditioned Indian

youth, last Thursday, which resulted in the death of Sir William Curzon Wyllie and also of Dr. Lalcaca.

(2) That this meeting considers it is due to the British public to assure them that they deplore with feelings of humiliation an act of this henious character committed in the metropolitan of the British Empire and beg that they will realise that it is the act of a fanatic and a mad man and it has aroused the deepest indignation of all the people of India.[23]

As these resolutions were put to vote and carried, some one from the centre of the hall jumped to his feet, and throwing his arms up, shouted, "No, No." He declared that he was not in agreement with the resolution. That was Savarkar and, for a while, there was absolute silence in the hall; but then two or three men rushed forward, and assaulted Savarkar, his eyeglasses were broken, and blood trickled from one of his eyes.[24] One Edward Palmer tried to eject Savarkar, but was struck by M.P. Tirumalacharya who had accompanied Savarkar to the meeting—and eventually both these men were thrown out of the meeting which proceeded thereafter smoothly. Khaparade who was present there gives a highly interesting eye-witness account of the whole dramatic episode.

...I intended going to Mr. Parikh's Chambers in the afternoon but Bipin Babu came and asked me to go with him to the Caxton Hall meeting convened by H.H. Aga Khan, Sir M. Bhownaggree and others. I did not like to refuse him. So we went to the Caxton Hall. There was a fairly large gathering of Indians and a sprinkling of Englishmen and women. The proceedings began in the usual way. I thought that H.H. Aga Khan was a scholar, but when he began to read from a manuscript and that also he could not read well, I came to know that his fame is in the keeping of his Secretary. The other speakers also made sorry figures. Syed Ameer Ali was a disappointment. When the first resolution was put, Savarkar objected to its wording. There was a tremendous uproar in the hall. Some people appear to have lost their heads. They cried "eject him, eject him." Mr. Morison who was sitting in front of me also joined in the cry, and there was a small scuffle. One east Indian came, his face bathed in blood and made a little speech saying his ancestors had helped in building up the Indian Empire. Later on Bipin Babu spoke and spoke very well. His was the speech of the evening. He and I left the meeting together, and took train to Hammersmith and thence walked to his house. Savarkar there told us that he objected to the words "crime" and "criminal" in the resolution, as an invasion of the province of courts....²⁵

Savarkar showed exemplary courage and ingeniousness in opposing the resolution in the Caxton Hall meeting where large number of people had assembled in order to denounce Dhingra's act. Savarkar was not made of the stuff to give in; he could swim against the tide, no matter what the price, and what the sacrifice. Probably there was no choice left for him, either. How could he be a party to the resolution which had branded Dhingra a criminal? What would Dhingra have thought of Savarkar if he had come to know that Savarkar was condemning his action? And what would have been his other associates reactions to this blatant vilification? But, by opposing these resolutions openly, he was exposing himself to the wrath of British authorities. Next day on 6 July Savarkar wrote a letter to *The Times* in which he said that nobody ought to be condemned unless found guilty. He pointed out that as the case was *sub judice*, the meeting had therefore no right to usurp the power of the Court by condemning Dhingra. He added further in the letter:

> The resolution was explained by those who proposed and seconded it, so as to presume the criminality of the man who is accused of having committed the murder. It seemed to me an encroachment upon the assumption of the authority of the Law Courts to declare a man who is still under trial to be a criminal. So it seemed to be more just and appropriate to omit the words "crime" and "criminals" from the resolution. As the proceedings had advanced too far to effect this, I simply voted against the resolution as it stood, and wanted to bring to the notice of the President the fact that the resolution could not be declared as passed unanimously.²⁶

Savarkar also announced in this letter that he would proceed against Palmer for assault.

Gokhale who represented the old guard had aversion to the revolutionaries of India House whose adventurous spirit and diatribes greatly upset him; but he chose to be reticent first, and made no comment on them as he thought that the young men of immature age and indisciplined emotions propagating violence would see the light of reason not before long. After Wyllie's murder, he could restrain himself no longer, and denounced publicly the philosophy of the bomb. Under the auspices of Deccan Sabha in Poona, he delivered a speech in Marathi, expressing the "horror and indignation on Wyllie's murder." He said: "The foul dead has blackened the Indian name and they must hang their head in shame before the whole civilised world."[27]

This speech by Gokhale was widely appreciated in the official circles, and Sir Edward Baker, the Lieutenant-Governor, Bengal, referred to it in complimentary terms in the Legislative Council of Bengal. He said:

> It would be well if all those now present and all the great audience outside, were to read, mark, learn and inwardly digest the forcible pronouncement which was made on this subject a few days ago by Gokhale at Poona. He has laid down with perfect clearness the lines on which the people of India must act if they desire to put a peremptory end to these ill-aimed atrocities whose only consequence must be the holding back of all the national achievement of the country.[28]

It is not necessary to discuss here Gokhale's political ideas but to emphasize that Gokhale strongly condemned Dhingra's act which he regarded as positively detrimental to the political advancement of India. He had warned Morley of the growth of wild and anarchical opinions among a section of Indian students in England.[29] In a note he explained his whole position with regard to the Indian revolutionaries in England including Dhingra. He wrote:

> During the last four years, I had to go three times to England and every time I discussed with growing anxiety the increased spread of Mr. Shamji Krishnavarma's ideas among a section of Indian students in London. I was, however, clinging to the hope that all that would pass away in a few years or so. I never spoke about this in India though I spoke about it to many youngmen themselves more than once at meetings in England. After Dhingra's crime, however, further reticence in the matter

became impossible. A reference to my speech will show that my object in speaking was two-fold—first to express the hope there would be no indiscriminate condemnation of Indian students in England and secondly to indicate to parents and guardians in the country the grave danger to which youngmen were exposed in England.[30]

Among Dhingra's critics, M.K. Gandhi was the severest of all; he was more elaborate and ruthless in his denunciation, and there was no trace of emotion in his attack. He had gone to England with H.O. Ali in a delegation sent to protest the notorious "Black Ordinance" requiring the registration of Asiatics and during his short stay there, Dhingra's case came up in the old Bailey. He sent back to Natal for publication in the *Indian Opinion* his views on Wyllie's murder. Gandhi made copious notes on Dhingra's act and ideology, and in his estimate found nothing worthy in any aspect of his performance. He believed that his own deputation's efforts to come to an understanding with the British received a serious set-back due to Dhingra's action which he feared was bound to change the attitude of British authorities from sympathy into antipathy. Gandhi was fearless in his analysis, and what he could never forgive was that Dhingra killed Wyllie when he was his guest. Gandhi wrote: "Wyllie was a guest of Association. From this point of view Madan Lal murdered his guest in his own house and killed Dr. Lalcaca who tried to interfere between them."[31]

According to Gandhi, Dhingra's murder of Wyllie had done immense harm to the cause of India's political aspirations. He regarded Dhingra's act as cowardly, and his defence, childish and absolutely unconvincing. He believed that Dhingra did not act on his own but was exploited by the machinations of others; even the statement which he presented in the Court was not his own— "some one else had written it." Gandhi thought that Dhingra had broken all norms, all rules, while performing the act; the rules, which according to Gandhi, even some of the worst criminals observe when they commit crimes. He criticized Dhingra on the following ground:

His [Dhingra's] defence is inadmissible. In my view he has acted like a coward. All the same one can pity the man. He was egged on to do this act by ill digested reading of worthless things.

His defence of himself too appears to have been learnt by rote. It is those who incited him to do so. In my view Dhingra was innocent. The murder was committed in a state of intoxication. It is not merely wine or bhang that makes one drunk; a mad idea can do so. That was the case with Dhingra.[32]

Surely, Gandhi was well-informed, and had heard of Dhingra's taking *bhang* before commiting the murder, but he raised the whole issue to the theoretical level of a mad idea. He also found Dhingra's statement praised otherwise for its lofty patriotism replete with false reasoning and analogies. Gandhi added:

The analogy of Germans and English is fallacious. If the Germans were to invade [British] the British would kill only the invaders. They would not kill every German or Germans, who are guests. If I kill someone in my house without a warning—some one who has done me no harm—I cannot but be called a coward. There is an ancient custom among the Arabs that they would not kill anyone in their own house; even if the person be their enemy. They would kill him, after he had left the house and after he had been given time to arm himself. Those who believe in violence would be brave men if they observe those rules when killing anyone. Otherwise they must be looked upon as cowards.[33]

Gandhi did not allow himself to be impressed by Dhingra's facing the gallows as a consequence of his act. He concedes that probably courage it was on his part, but courage expended in a wrong way. Gandhi argued:

It may be said that what Dhingra did publicly and knowing full well that he himself would have to die augurs courage of no mean order on his part. But as I have said above men can do nothing in a state of intoxication and can also banish the fear of death. Whatever courage there is in this is the result of intoxication, not a quality of the man himself. A man's courage consists in suffering deeply and over a long period. That alone is a brave act which is preceded by careful reflection. Those who believe in this madness are ignorant, who will rule in their place—murderers. India can gain nothing from this rule of murders. I am afraid some Indians will commend this murder. I believe they will be guilty of a henious crime.[34]

Condemning the use of violence in political strategy, Gandhi wrote: "One of the accepted and time-bound methods to attain the end is that of violence. The assassination of Sir Curzon Wyllie was an illustration in its worst and [most] detestable form of that method."[35]

Gandhi firmly believed that Dhingra's sacrifice was futile, calculated to do immense harm to Indian's political struggle. He warned:

> Those who believe that India has gained by Dhingra's act and and other similar act in India made a serious mistake. Dhingra was a patriot but his mistaken love was blind. He gave his body in a wrong way; its ultimate result was mischievous.[36]

It would be clear from the extracts given above that Gandhi was not willing to consider Dhingra a hero, but a misguided youth who under the intoxication of *bhang* or some mad idea was incited by the wily designs of others to destroy his own life for a purely fruitless and ill-fated pursuit.

Syed Amir Ali, a leading member of the London branch of the All India Muslim League in 1908-1913, called Dhingra's act a "national disaster."[37]

In India too there was widespread manifestation of horror against Dhingra's murder of Wyllie.[38] The All India Congress Committee, Lahore, under the chairmanship of Sheikh Umar Baksh, passed a resolution condemning the "senseless and dastardly act of Dhingra."[39] Pandit Madan Mohan Malaviya criticized Dhingra's act and said, "I am grieved the more to think he should have been a Hindu."[40] The rising politically ambitious young men in Punjab like Harkishan Lal and Mohd. Shafi denounced Dhingra's act; even Malik Umar Hyat Khan who at one time had been associated with Savarkar and the India House went to the extent of describing Savarkar and his other associates as "low-caste men."[41] There is no doubt that the dominant Indian political elite deprecated Dhingra's act, and this attitude of the political leadership criticizing Dhingra was warmly commended by the

Under Secretary, The Master of Elibank, in the House of Commons:

> We may safely say that amidst all the froth and foam of a few maliciously inclined seditionists, who are held in contempt by the loyal population, the mass of the people of India remain unmoved, are fully sensible to the material improvement in their conditions.[42]

The diary and the correspondence of Dunlop Smith contain certain letters which throw valuable light on the attitude of the British authorities towards Dhingra's action. King Edward VII was deeply agitated over Wyllie's murder, and wanted the Viceroy, Lord Minto, to take such drastic steps as to deter the Indian youth from following Dhingra's unfortunate example. The King wrote:

> Serious steps should be taken to prevent these men coming over to England with no fixed occupation, and falling into bad hands which they invariably do. They only learn sedition and treason, which they infuse into the minds of their countrymen both in England and in India. What can one, however, expect if such a soundrel as Keir Hardie, who is also a member of the House of Commons, foment sedition in India and at home against our mode of Government? The harm he has done is incalculable—and makes one's blood boil.[43]

Morley declined to take a lenient view of Dhingra's crime despite the Dhingra family's requests and explanations, and thought the death penalty just the right punishment for him. Morley wrote to Minto:

> [Madan Lal's] execution may lean to retaliation and blood-feud, not only against us in the India Office, but against lonely Europeans in remote places in India itself. But be that as it may, we hang a murderer when we are lucky enough to catch one, and so we shall hang Dhingra. I am not in love with Indian affairs all the same. Are you?[44]

Lady Minto's journal records that the Nawab of Loharu, Sir Amir-ud-Din Ahmad Khan, went to the length of suggesting to

The Impact

Minto that for Dhingra's act, his entire family ought to be exterminated. Lady Minto describes with her usual *sang-froid* the interview which the Nawab had with the Viceroy on the subject:

> The Nawab of Loharu . . . is quite up to date with his ideas, with the exception of the way he considers malefactors should be dealt with. The Dhingra family, he said, should be exterminated. "But", argued Rolly, "Dhingra's father and brothers are most loyal, respectable members of society and they are not responsible for the action of one member and of their family". Loharu raised both hands to his face and said: "That cannot be helped. It is their misfortune, and they must suffer as an example of the public. That is the will of God". No oriental can understand our view of justice, and it all seems contrary to the customs of their race to show mercy and pity.[45]

King Edward had suggested in his letter to Minto that the influence of Keir Hardie in the dissemination of seditionary ideas among Indian students was quite pronounced, and probably it was due to Keir Hardie's propaganda that a large number of placards were posted throughout Ireland, praising the heroism of Dhingra who had laid down his life for the honour of his country. [46] But these posters were eventually removed by the police.

It has been suggested that Shyamji Krishnavarma, the founder of India House who ought to have felt really proud of Dhingra's act—as it seemed to have translated into reality his long cherished hopes—denounced his act unreasonably;[47] but his biographer does not give any evidence in support of this statement. On the other hand, the biographer adds that the "nationalist friends and colleagues beseiged Krishnavarma with angry and scathing comments";[48] and it was only under this discomfiting pressure that he was forced to praise Dhingra's act. Krishnavarma's reticence at this moment was quite understandable because to expose himself at this moment when suspicion and fear were rife might have created problems for himself, his associates, and his property in London. A successful revolutionary is one who is sensitive to a degree that he does not allow himself to be detected; others run after to trap him, but they too fail. But finally Shyamji chose to write a letter to *The Times* regretting Wyllie's death, and then justifying the use of violence for the political struggle of his countrymen:

Allow me to say at the very outset that on personal grounds I regret the death of Sir Curzon Wyllie, whom I had the pleasure of first meeting 22 years ago when I was Dewan or Chief Minister of Rutlam. For nearly five years he and I had amicable official relations at Udaipur where I, as a member of the State Council, had amongst other duties the charge of the political department. ... A letter written by him before I left England for good in 1907 he commenced by addressing me "Dear Mr. Shyam" and ended "some time has passed since I last saw you, I trust that you are getting on well."[49]

But the most eloquent tribute to Dhingra was paid by that firebrand intellectual revolutionary, Har Dayal who said:

Dhingra has behaved at each stage of his trial like a hero of ancient times. He has reminded us of the history of medieval Rajputs and Sikhs who loved death like a bride. England thinks she killed Dhingra: in reality he lives forever, and has given the deathblow to English sovereignty in India. In time to come, when the British Empire in India shall have been reduced to dust and ashes, Dhingra's monument will adorn the squares of our chief towns, recalling the memory of our children to the noble life and the noble death of him who laid down his life in a far-off land for the cause he loved so well.[50]

But less than five years later, Har Dayal had to say things different about Dhingra:

I will give you my estimate and you can take it for what is worth. He was a morbid, melancholy and indolent man; very susceptible to personal influence and very very unbalanced, very vain; and unwilling to exert himself for a successful career. This is my idea of him.[51]

Why should Har Dayal have attacked Dhingra so fiercely four years after he had praised him sky-high, it is difficult to say for want of material evidence. After all, Dhingra had approximated to the ideal of a true revolutionary, but this denigration which provides a psychological insight into his personality, though unexpected, was rather personal, and not from the point of view of Indian

The Impact

nationalism. From the British side, W.S. Blunt, the supporter of the Egyptian, Irish, and Indian nationalist movements, and opponent of British Imperialism, expressed admiration for Dhingra's action, and wrote: "No christian martyr ever faced his judges more fiercely or with greater dignity. Blunt has given a graphic account of his meeting with Winston Churchill and their frank exchange of views on Dhingra."[52] Blunt added:

> Again we sat up till later. Among the many memorable things Churchill said was this: Talking of Dhingra he said that there had been much discussion in the Cabinet about him. Llyod George had expressed to him his highest admiration on Dhingra's attitude as a patriot, in which he [Churchill] shared. He [Dhingra] will be remembered 2,000 years hence, as we remember Regulus and Caractacus and Plutarch's heroes, and Churchill quoted with admiration Dhingra's last words as the finest ever made in the name of patriotism.[53]

The English press was outraged at Wyllie's assassination, and was "united in its religious horror at the crime." But Blunt condemned the partisan role of the press as highly unjustified, and completely opposed to its former claims and professions. Blunt pointed out how the English press had "applauded exactly such crimes in Italy fifty years ago and in Russia the other day."

Blunt also has recorded in his diary a discussion he had about Dhingra with Lyne Stevens, a friend of the King which is as follows:

> [He] Stevens talked about the Dhingra assassination, which seems to have at last convinced his Royal friends that there is something wrong about the state of India. People talk about political assassination as defeating its own end, but that is nonsense. It is just the stock needed to convince selfish rulers that selfishness has its limits of impudence. It is like that other fiction that England never yields to threats. My experience is that when England has her face well slapped then she apologises, never before.[54]

In a speech Victor Grayson, Socialist MP, while referring to Wyllie's murder said that:

He had that morning seen a portrait of the murderer, whom they called an assassin, and he said to himself why not put Lord Morley in and say another assassin. He did not condone the act, but extended his sympathy to the poor Indian, mad and exasperated by the horrors endured by his people.[55]

It would be clear from the evidence cited above that the dominant sentiment burst forth against Dhingra's assassination of Wyllie. The British Government was determined to take drastic action against Dhingra, and settle the whole issue in furious haste without allowing his rivals to make political capital out of it. John Morley, Secretary of State for India, enjoyed the reputation of a staunch liberal who in the administration of the affairs of state would probably ask: "What are the principles involved?" and not "what are the chances of its success?" He wished to treat Dhingra's case as a single and isolated act, and not a part of conspiracy because it was always his policy to advise proceedings for sedition when a conviction was reasonably certain.[56] When the Home authorities saw that on a recent occasion, of 2,000 cases submitted for his opinion, an Advocate-General advised proceedings only in a dozen of them, Morley taunted: "What a sensible example."[57] It was suggested to him to try Dhingra privately, but this suggestion Morley rejected with his mock derision.

I was amazed to hear—urge upon me that we should try Dhingra privately [the murderer of a poor Wyllie] so as to prevent the public dissemination of his poisonous froth. Excellent, I daresay —only to hang a man after a trial in camera![58]

The strain of pacifism and radical idealism was a genuine part of Morley's composition. James Campbell Ker, Personal Assistant to the Director of Criminal Intelligence, stated:

... the whole circumstances leave little doubt that the murder of an Englishman was planned by Savarkar in revenge for the sentence passed on his brother, and that the particular victim was chosen to satisfy the private grudge of Krishnavarma![59]

A highly intelligent, tenacious, and influential man like Morley could not be indifferent to the hectic political activity under the leadership of Savarkar in India House. Now that the outrage was committed, what was he to do? His sound political instinct guided him to go slow. According to Fredrick Arthur Hirtzel who has provided interesting material in his diary on Wyllie's assassination, Morley was "inclined to pooh pooh any suggestion for facilitating inquiry into what was going on in India."[60] Morley had declared that he "has never seen a particle of evidence during the last two years pointing to a conspiracy."[61] Therefore in the conditioning circumstances, Morley had decided to "keep cool and engender a spirit of calm sanity among those around him."[62] If Morley had treated Dhingra's case as a part of conspiracy, then surely the issue would have assumed a wider dimension and produced a far more complicated situation. What suited Morley most was the extradition of Indian revolutionaries from the highly sensitive and political conscious atmosphere of London. In England a man involved in seditionary activities could get two or three years' imprisonment, but in India, the story was different where the administrative machinery rode roughshod. As subsequent events showed Morley's handling of the situation was politic because it liquidated the political activity in India House.

The dominant Indian political opinion assailed Dhingra's action: those views were most forcefully expressed by Gokhale and Gandhi; but it must be recognized that quite a large number of political leaders including Gandhi were impressed by Dhingra's courage, though they firmly believed that the type of courage displayed by Dhingra was expended in a wrong way. Khaparde had publicly deprecated Dhingra's action, but later he praised his heroic qualities. Blunt wrote: "He [Khaparde] is as full of as I am of Dhingra's courage. We agreed that if India could produce five hundred men as absolutely without fear she would achieve her freedom."[63]

It is something of a puzzle that the extremists did not acclaim publicly Dhingra's heroism; only a few revolutionaries and close associates of Dhingra waxed lyrical over the record of his "imperishable services" to the liberation of his country.

After Dhingra's assassination of Wyllie, India House was closed, and it ceased to be resort for Indians; and Krishnavarma sold it away. As a consequence of murder of Jackson, the District Magistrate of Nasik, Savarkar sought refuge in Paris on 6 January 1910; returned to England on 13 March, was arrested, and sent to

India. V.V.S. Aiyer and Virendra Chattopadhyaya shifted to Paris, H.K. Koregaonkar and Chatturbhaj turned approvers in the Nasik conspiracy case, Harnam Singh had already deserted his friends under domestic pressure, Bapat was in India. Dhingra was executed. And henceforth, not London, but Paris became the centre of revolutionary activities with Aiyer, S.R. Rana, Har Dayal, and Rajput of Kathiawar as leaders.

6 Epilogue

History is a concrete interpretation of human action fixed in time and place, but its course is usually tortuous and unpredictable, and things do not happen in it as they are fancied. The entire story of Madan's emergence into a militant nationalist, and his assassination of Sir Curzon Wyllie shows that the results were invariably the exact opposite of what was intended. Could anyone imagine that Dhingra, who belonged to a rich family that always pledged its loyalty to the British Government, would ever turn into a revolutionary, and kill their family friend Wyllie? Dhingra had become almost an intractable problem to his family because of his erratic behaviour, and it was thought proper to send him abroad with the hope that the change in climate and atmosphere would reform him and establish him in some honourable profession; but that was not to be, as the subsequent course of events showed. Dhingra went to England for higher studies, but politics for which he had no interest in India became his dominant passion in England—by habit he was an Anglicist, though in action an inverterate foe of the British. Almost at every turn of his experience, he was overtaken by surprises, unexpectedness, and situations of paradoxical character.

It is clear from the evidence available that Dhingra had set his mind on killing Lord Morley or Lord Curzon. He had been haunting for either of them for about six months. It has been suggested that Dhingra while killing Wyllie believed him to be Lord Curzon, and this assumption rests largely on the confusion which their common names creates. To say the least, this is a grotesque suggestion. Dhingra was a highly educated person, politically conscious, and being a regular visitor to India House in London, and a close associate of Savarkar, it is incredible that he could not distinguish one from the other. Curzon Wyllie was a friend of the Dhingra family whom Madan had known since his childhood, and was introduced to him by his elder brother Kundan Lal in London. In his letter Wyllie had asked Madan Lal Dhingra to meet him; and probably they met. But the more important aspect of the matter is that Dhingra though determined to kill Morley or Curzon proved unsuccessful in his mission, but had to kill Wyllie not of choice but out of the force of circumstances mainly because Savarkar and his associates' pressure on him was irresistible. Dhingra had no intention of killing Dr Lalcaca who interposed himself between Wyllie and Dhingra; his death was an accident. Dhingra tried to shoot himself but failed—he had used all the bullets, and thus was forced to pass through the ordeal of execution and all that nerve-racking experience which preceded it, and which he had wanted to avoid. Here is another specimen of the irony of history which plays tricks with men's plans.

In India House, times were marked by high enthusiasm and novelty of enterprise—it was no sluggish or quiet era. Savarkar had roused the young men to a deeper and true interest in their country. The majority of the India House revolutionaries were between 16 and 25 years old, and most of them were students and teachers, and some of them had recently been called to the bar, quite a few of them had failed in the ICS but all of them were high-caste Hindus, either Brahmins or Kayasthas of rich and middle-class families. There was widespread resentment among them because of the humiliations they had suffered at the hands of the British authorities, and they remained sulking, and chose underground revolutionary activities. By following the examples of the Russian intelligentsia, they launched an anarchist movement modelled on the Russian revolutionaries, and aimed at the subversion of the existing government.

These young men believed that the political problem of India could not be solved by reason or debate. They dismissed the Moderates as naive, ritualistic, and shallow. They were determined to sweep away the politics of lassitude, and inaugurate the politics of hope. They were ideologists in the broadest and loosest sense; their oratory dealt in mood and programme, and with inspired eccleticism they drew on all types and sources for their ideas and policies from the Russian nihilists to the *Adi Granth* of the Sikhs. They were uncertain, but expectant, despondent but hopeful, troubled but sanguine. At bottom they were seeking a new articulation of national values. It seemed as though the wind was beginning to change; there was a new sense of purpose and commitment, looking for a feeling of dedication. New forces, new energies, and new values were stirring for expression. Savarkar's *The Indian War of Independence, 1857* was a symptom of the felt need for some kind of spiritual and moral affirmation.

Dhingra had had a gloomy childhood. His parents' high standard of obedience and achievement was in some instance more a burden than an encouragement, far less an inspiration, and he chafed under the restraints of life. He is reported to have been scolded on occasions by his formidable father who brooked no opposition, but Madan was eager to establish and maintain his independence. He appears to have drifted through life, and to have been shunted about by circumstances which he could neither foresee nor control. The crockery of his feelings was damaged, and there was agonizing dislocation in certain vital aspects of his life.

He had the habit of pinching children just to hurt them. The boy who torments another boy, "for no reason" is pleased, with his victim's pain, not from any disinterested love of evil or pleasure in pain but mainly because this pain is a clear proof of his own powers over his victims. Dhingra's thwarted sense of superiority which had developed since his childhood wanted satisfaction. He felt the excitement of one who, being fearless in nature, executed a feat only just within his compass which was congenial to his special aptitude.

The fact that Dhingra ran away from home the next day after his marriage[1] raises certain important issues which cannot be settled for want of evidence, but such behaviour immediately after marriage is rather curious as it demonstrates lack of absolute confidence to face the reality of things, a kind of escapism joined with a feeling of self-assertion and rebellion. If he left his home due to impotence whether physical or psychological,[2] then such a state of utter incapacity and its exposition, while on the one hand, tends to make one conscious of his disabilities, on the other, it boils up the inner drives to a high pressure to do something momentous. In such moments of psychological crisis, man sometimes tries to over-reach himself. Actions arise out of specific needs and frustrations.

Dhingra felt alienated, and was a repressed individual who had bottled up his feelings until they welled forth in a torrent. A psychiatrist may find in him something of an aggressive psychopath who was physically violent and quite indifferent to the rights and feelings of others, and who showed little remorse or regret after such a behaviour. According to medical opinion, individuals like Dhingra, lacking in persistence are often charming but feckless.[3] Life gets dull for them, and in their mood of depression and gloom, only some episode of aggressive behaviour clears the air and relieves the tension and monotony. Dhingra became so embedded in the social environment of India House that it was not possible for him to retreat and change his pattern of behaviour. In such circumstances, some external force was to provide an outrageous stimulation.

It is not intended here to import the technical language of psychoanalysis into this discussion, but it has been shown that the irrational devotion which an individual shows to a leader (like Dhingra to Savarkar) is simply a transference of an emotional relationship which has been dissolved or repressed within the family circle. Because of his alienation with the world, Dhingra seemed to have transfered all sorts of imaginary virtues to Savarkar, which he himself would have liked to possess. Savarkar's association with Dhingra stands prominent among the causes at the very least, among the signals of a great change in the entire political outlook. In the case of the study of revolutionaries it has to be emphasized that they start from their own concern and work outward rather than start from the national needs and work inwards.

Dhingra's action was generally condemned in Indian political circles, though there was a strong feeling of admiration for his courage. Such a public reaction was also unexpected. Even the staunch and intrepid nationalists had reservations about his method. The young revolutionaries of India House had hoped that Dhingra's act would intensify the revolutionary campaign against the British, but these hopes were belied, and the immediate results were just the opposite. The India House was closed, and the firebrand revolutionaries scattered. Despite the lofty idealism, high enthusiasm, and feverish political activity, these young men in India House did not know what they were really after; they did not really proceed upon any well-formulated plan. Still less had they any idea of the lengths to which they were fated to go, nor could they always explain afterwards how they had been brought to advance so far. Being young and inexperienced, they lacked the maturity and skill to sustain an ideology or a programme. With

Epilogue

the removal of Savarkar from the scene, the bottom of the whole organization dropped out. But Dhingra's example of courage became a part of Indian rhetoric, and often was cited later as a case of supreme sacrifice for the liberation of India. The Gandhian politics which dominated the Indian scene later expelled the use of force from its ideology, and declared non-violence as its creed. That is why the philosophy of the bomb preached by Savarkar and followed by Dhingra found only a few of its adherents in the national struggle. The tide of Indian political ideology flowed in a different direction altogether.

APPENDIXES

APPENDIX

Appendix I

OH MARTYRS

The battle of freedom once begun
And handed down from sire to son
Though often lost is ever won;

To-day is the tenth of May; it was on this day, that in the ever memorable year of 1857, the first campaign of the War of Independence was opened by you. Oh Martyrs, on the battlefield of India. The Motherland awakened to the sense of her honour. It was on this day that the war-cry *"Maro Feringhee Ko"* was raised by the throats of thousands. It was on this day that the sepoys of Meerut having risen in a terrible uprising, marched down to Delhi, saw the waters of the Jumna, glittering in the sunshine, caught one of those historical moments which close past epoch to introduce a new one, and "had found, in a moment, a leader, a flag and a cause and converted the mutiny into a national and a religious war."

This day therefore we dedicate, Oh Martyrs, to your inspiring memory. It was on this day that you raised a new flag to be upheld, you uttered a mission to be fulfilled, you saw a vision to be realised, you proclaimed a nation to be born.

We take up your cry, we revere your flag, we are determined to continue that fiery mission of "away with the foreigner" which you uttered, amidst the prophetic thunderings of the Revolutionary war. For the War of 1857 shall not cease till the revolutionary arrives, striking slavery into dust, elevating liberty to the throne. Whenever a people rises for its freedom, whenever that seed of liberty gets germinated in the blood of its father and whenever there remains at least one true son to avenge that blood of his father there never can be end to such a war as this. No, a revolutionary war knows not truce, save liberty or death. We inspired by your memory, determine to continue the struggle you began in 1857, we look upon the battles you fought as the battles of the first campaign the defeat of which cannot be the defeat of the war. What? Shall the world say that India has accepted the defeat as the final one? That the blood of 1857 was shed in vain? No, by Hindusthan, no; the historical continuity of the Indian nation is not cut off. The war began on the 10th of May 1857 is not over on the 10th of May 1908, nor shall it ever cease till a 10th of May-to-come sees the destiny accomplished, sees the beautiful Ind crowned. But O glorious Martyrs, in this pious struggle of your sons, help. Torn in innumerable petty selves, we cannot realise the grand unity of the Mother. Whisper, then, unto us by what magic you caught the secret of union. How the Feringhee rule was shattered to pieces and the Swadeshi thrones were set up by the common consent of Hindus and Mahomedans. How in the higher love of the Mother, united the difference of castes and creeds, how the venerated and venerable Bahadur Shah prohibited the killing of cows throughout India. How Shreemant Nanasahib after the first salute of the thundering cannon to the emperor of Delhi, reserved for himself the second one! How you staggered the whole world by uniting under the banner of mother and forced your enemies to say: "Among the many lessons the Indian Mutiny conveyed to the historians and administrators, none is of greater importance than the warning that it is possible to have a revolution in which Brahmins and Shudras, Mohemedans and Hindus were united against us and that it is not safe to suppose that the peace and stability of our dominion in any great measure depends on the continent being inhabited by different races with different religious systems, for they mutually understand each other and respect and take part in each other's modes and ways and doings. The Mutiny reminds us that our dominions rest on a thin crust ever likely to be rent by titanic fires of social changes and revolutions!"

And give us the marvellous energy, dare and secrecy with which you organized the mighty volcano; show us the volcanic magma that underlie the green thin crust on which the foe is to be kept lulled into a false security; tell us how the Chapati, that fiery cross of India flew from village to village and from valley to valley setting the whole intellect of the nation on fire by the very vagueness of its message and then let us hear the roaring thunder with which the volcano at last burst forth an all-shattering force rushing, smashing, burning and consuming into one continuous fiery flow of red-hot lava-flood! Within a month, regiment after regiment, Prince after Prince, city after city, sepoys, police, Zamindars, Pandits, Moulvis, the multiple-headed Revolution sounded its tocsin and temples and mosques resounded with the cry *"Maro Feringhee Ko"* (Away with the foreigners). Meerut rose, Delhi rose, rose Benaras, Agra, Patna, Lucknow, Allahabad, Jagadalpore, Jhansi, Banda, Indore—from Peshawar to Calcutta and from the Narmada to the Himalayas, the volcano burst forth into a sudden, simultaneous and all consuming conflagration.

And then, Oh Martyrs, tell us the little as well as the great defects which you found out in our people in that great experiment of yours. But above all, point out that most ruinous, nay, the only material draw-back in the body of the nation which rendered all your efforts futile, the mean selfish blindness which refuses to see its way to join the nation's cause. Say that the only cause of the defeat of Hindusthan was Hindusthan herself, that shaking away the slumbers of centuries, the mother rose to hit the foe, but while her right hand was striking the Feringhees dead, her left hand struck, alas not the enemy, but her own fore-head! So she staggered and fell back into the inevitable swoon of 50 years.

Fifty years are past, but oh restless hearts, behold that your Diamond Jubilee shall not pass without seeing your wishes fulfilled. The Duab and Ayodhya making a united stand, waged a war not only against the whole of the British power but against the rest of India too, and yet you fought for three years and yet you had wellnigh snatched away the crown of Hindusthan and smashed the hollow existence of the alien rule. What an encouragement this! What the Duab and Ayodhya could do in a month, the simultaneous sudden and determined rising of the whole of Hindusthan can do in a day. This hope illumines our hearts and assures us of success. And so we allow that your Diamond Jubilee year 1917 shall not pass without seeing and resurging Ind making a triumphant entry into the world. For, the bones of Bahadur Shah are crying vengeance from their grave. The spirit of Mangal Panday is still betokening from the scaffold for the fulfilment of the sacred mission. The solemn affirmation of Kumar Singh to shatter to pieces the British rule is still echoing in the air of Hindusthan. The streaks of blood that flowed from Azim-Ullah and Pir Ali Shah have left an indelible impression on the pages of history. For, Veer Tatia Tope when he was going to the gallows for having refused to admit his "crime" said in prophetic words, "You may hang me today, you may hang such as me every day, but thousands will still rise in my place, your object will never be gained."

Indians, these words must be fulfilled! Your blood, Oh Martyrs, shall be avenged.

VANDE MATARAM

NOTE: This speech was delivered by Savarkar on the 50th Anniversary of 1857.

Appendix II

Puggaree Sambhal O Jatta!
Puggaree Sambhal Oye!
Faslan nun Kha Gaya Kide;
Tan te nahin tere lide;
Bhukhan ne Khub napide;
Ronde nen bal oye!
Puggaree Sambhal O Jatta!
Puggaree Sambhal Oye!
Hind hai mandir tera,
Is da Pujari tun!
Kad tak Jhallenga tun
ehdi Khwari nun?
Ladan te maran di
Kar lai tyari tun
Puggari Sambhal O Jatta!
Puggari Sambhal Oye!

The English rendering of this song is as follows:

O brother peasant, take care of your turban!
O, take care of your turban!
Insects have devoured your crops;
There are no rags even on your body;
Hunger has sucked you while;
your children cry for bread oh!
O Brother peasant, take care of your turban!
O, take care of your turban!
India is your temple,
And you are her priest,
How long will you brook these insults?
Be prepared for a battle of death,
O Brother peasant, take care of your turban!
O, take care of your turban!

Appendix III

One could perhaps appreciate better why Jawaharlal Nehru went into politics if one sees how dominated by a formidable father, he found an outlet in rebelling not against his father which he dared not do but against the system of British rule which represented oppression.

Some time ago a prominent political leader who wishes to remain unidentified told this writer how Jinnah became determined to adopt an uncompromising attitude on the solution of India's political problem. Though to explain the whole of the Partition of India and Jinnah's fanatical obstinacy on the basis of the following incident would be an over-simplification; this account shows how psychological factors do play a vital part in the formation of ideas and attitudes. When Jinnah left India for London, and started practising at the Privy Council Bar in 1931, someone close to both men told Nehru that Jinnah had left India for good; and Nehru is reported to have said sharply, "Good riddance." This cryptic and severe comment was conveyed to Jinnah who reacted sharply, and wanted Nehru to be informed that he was now determined to return to India, and teach people like him a lesson of their lives. Jinnah returned to India and tried to undo what Nehru stood for.

This story was confirmed by the late Dr Syed Mahmud, a close friend of Nehru, who had been also on cordial terms with Jinnah's beautiful wife Rattenbai.

Appendix IV

This writer learnt about Madan Lal Dhingra's marriage from his nephew Mukand Lal Dhingra, a resident of Amritsar. On being questioned about this source of information, Mukand Lal said that his grandmother (Madan Lal's mother) had mentioned it to him. The story current in the family is that Madan ran away from home the next day after his marriage. Why he took such an unusual course, it is rather difficult to say due to lack of evidence, but this much is certain that Madan's wife was married again by his father after Madan's death. Probably Madan had sent a message to his father from Brixton prison to marry off his wife. For a man of Sahib Ditta's means and influence, it was no problem to find a husband for a young widow. It is believed that she got married to a barrister from Sargodha (West Punjab).

Madan Lal's other nephew, Dr H.L. Dhingra, a well-known dentist in Delhi, confirms the above story. H.L. Dhingra was about seven or eight years old when Madan had left for England, and has faint recollections of his uncle. He said that he used to call Madan's wife *chachi*, meaning aunt. According to him, she was quite good-looking, and was later married to some barrister in Lyallpur or Montegomery. Madan's niece, Mrs Shukla Hari Das (an Oxford graduate living now in Simla), wrote in a letter to this writer, dated 25 July 1977: "I did hear that Madan Lal Dhingra was got married before he went to England, but I never heard there was a son."

After Madan's execution in Pentonveille Prison, London, on 17 August 1909, Sahib Ditta made the following entry in his diary:

Though misguided but firm and determined, my beloved seventh child in order of birth will not be in this world today. Most unfortunate day for me. Bereaved father.

Sahib Ditta Mal Dhingra

It is a pity that Sahib Ditta's diary which recorded his daily impressions is not available. Mukand Lal possessed this diary for long until it was lost, but he remembers the above quoted lines. Madan's execution produced a great change in his father who became a sad man. While returning from Srinagar to Amritsar he died on the way in a car accident near Domel between Srinagar and Rawalpindi on 29 October 1916. His memorial in the Ram Bagh gardens bears:

Born 30th of July, 1846
Dead 29 October 1916.

In his registered will, Sahib Ditta stipulated that none of his family members could claim any financial assistance from his Trust for proceeding to England.

The British Government recognized Sahib Ditta's services to the government by allowing his sons to build a memorial in Ram Bagh, a rare privilege given to an individual—in the middle of the garden there is Maharaja Ranjit Singh's luxurious two-storeyed summer capital.

NOTES

CHAPTER 1

[1] Madan Lal Dhingra's date and place of birth are still uncertain. The Madan Lal Dhingra Memorial Committee, appointed by the Punjab Government to identify Madan's date and place of birth, and comprising Gurbax Rai Sethi, Dr Sant Ram Seth, and Sadhu Ram (well-informed on the local history of Amritsar), could not come to any conclusion. The Dhingra family's genealogical chart which is in the possession of Madan's nephew Mukand Lal is moth-eaten; so, the date is illegible. The Municipal Records at Amritsar listing dates of birth and death perished during the Political Disturbances of 1919. According to *The Tribune*, Lahore, 4 July 1909, Madan was twenty-two in 1909, which dates his birth as 1887.

[2] According to the present calculations, the assets would amount approximately to Rs 63,60,000. Sahib Ditta was the first Indian in Amritsar to own a car; he had six carriages driven by horses which were housed in *Baggi-Khana*, especially built for the purpose.

[3] The main source of information of Madan's early life is the joint letter addressed by his elder brothers, Dr Mohan Lal Dhingra and Dr Behari Lal Dhingra, to the Private Secretary to the Viceroy. See Government of India, Home Department, *Proceedings*, Political A, September 1909, Nos. 66-68, Appendix (letter from Dr Mohan Lal, M.D. and Dr Behari Lal Dhingra, M.D. to the Private Secretary to the Viceroy, Simla, dated 7 July 1909). The members of the Dhingra family have provided additional information. B.S. Maighowalia's pamphlet, *First Indian Martyr Executed in Pentonevilla Prison, London,* using the British newspapers, provides an interesting account which is descriptive, than explanatory. See Brahma Nath Datta, *The Martyrdom of Madan Lal Dhingra: Amar Saheed Madan Lal Dhingra*, pp. 3-8; S.C. Mittal, "Vafadar Pita Ka Krantikari Putra," *Jan Pradeep*, 1 July 1968; A.K. Deshpande, *Hutatma: Madan Lal Dhingra*. See V.N. Datta, "Madan Lal Dhingra Through Contemporary Eyes," *The Tribune*, 14 December 1976.

[4] *The Tribune*, 6 July 1909.

[5] Government of India, Home Department, *Proceedings*, Political A, September 1909, Nos. 66-78. The question of Madan's eccentricity will be discussed later; this trait of eccentricity in him was mentioned by his family after he had killed Sir William Curzon Wyllie mainly with the object of

persuading the British Government to take a compassionate view on his action.

[6] *Lascar* means an Indian sailor. *The Tribune*, 14 July 1909.

[7] Government of India, Home Department, *Proceedings*, Political A, September 1909, Nos. 66-68.

[8] V.N. Datta, *Amritsar: Past and Present*, pp. 45-49.

[9] Rash Behari Bose (1880/6-1945). Born in 1880 in Subaldha (Burdwan) or in 1886 in Parale-Bighati (Hoogly); an associate of the great revolutionary, Aurbindo Ghosh; joined the Forest Research Institute, Dehradun, as clerk; was connected with the terrorist activities in Delhi, Punjab, and Bengal; planned a general rising in Northern India on 21 February 1915 which failed; evaded arrest, and managed to escape to Japan, where he founded in 1924 the Indian Independence League; formed the Indian National Army during the Second World War which he handed over to Subash Chander Bose in June 1943; and died in Tokyo on 21 January 1945.

[10] Ghadr: A revolutionary organization originally known as the "Hindustan Association of the Pacific Coast" was established in the USA; its official organ, the *Ghadr*, began to be published as a weekly from 1 November 1913, and because of the journal, the organization came to be known as the Ghadr Party. Its object was to overthrow the British Raj through the use of violence. With the outbreak of the First World War, it gained momentum largely due to the return of the Japanese merchantship, the Komagata Maru, which was not allowed to land at Vancouver. The night of 21 February 1915 was fixed for raising the standard of rebellion in India. Rash Bihari Bose and Vishnu Ganesh Pingley had master-minded the revolutionary activities of the party, but the whole plan of the revolutionaries was smashed by the quick action on the part of the government, and lack of maintaining secrecy by the revolutionaries about their programme.

[11] Sachin Sanyal (1895-1945). He formed a revolutionary group round 1908 which trained the youth in wrestling and gymnastics and was known later as Young Men's Association. He came in touch with Rash Bihari Bose who converted him to his ideology of using violence for political ends; was closely associated with the uprising of 21 February 1915 which failed; and he was sentenced to transportation for life, and deported to the Andamans.

[12] Vishnu Ganesh Pingley (1888-1915): Born in 1888 at Telegoan Dhandhere in Poona District, went to the USA in 1911, where he came to know the revolutionary leader, Har Dyal; returned to India in 1914, threw himself into the revolutionary movement and tried to induce the Indian soldiers to join in the general rising against the British; visited the cantonments at Lahore, Ambala, Ferozepur, Rawalpindi, and Meerut; was arrested on 23 March 1915 with a tin box containing ten bombs; was tried in the Lahore Conspiracy Case and hanged on 17 November 1915 in the Lahore Central jail.

[13] Paaray Mohan, *An Imaginary Rebellion*, p. 60.

[14] V.N. Datta, *op. cit.*, pp. 45-49.

[15] V.N. Datta, *Jallianwala Bagh*, pp. 63-64.

Notes

16. Martin Gilbert, *Servant of India*, p. 188.
17. *Ibid.*, see also Countess of Lady Minto, *India: Minto and Morley*, p. 320.
18. Muzaffurpur Bomb Case. Two bombs were thrown on 30 April 1908 by Prafulla Chaki and Khudi Ram Bose on two ladies, the Kennedys, the mother and daughter, which were really meant for Kingsford, the District Judge, who had gained great unpopularity among Indians due to his vindictive judgement, particularly in having sentenced Bipin Chandra Pal to six months rigorous imprisonment. Prafulla Chaki tried to escape, but was shot dead; and Khudi Ram Bose was hanged.
19. This letter was sent to the Viceroy as evidence to emphasize the loyalty of the Dhingra family to the British Raj. See Government of India, Home Department, *Proceedings*, Political A, September 1909, Nos. 66-68. Enclosures, Extracts of a letter from Chuni Lal Dhingra (May 1908).
20. *Ibid.*, Note by Dunlop Smith to the Viceroy, 7 July 1909.
21. *Ibid.*, see also Gilbert, *op. cit.*, p. 192.

CHAPTER 2

1. Interview with Mukand Lal Dhingra, 5 July 1977. See Government of India, Home Department, *Proceedings*, Political A, September 1909, Nos. 66-68, Letter from Dr Mohan Lal Dhingra and Dr Behari Lal Dhingra to the Private Secretary to the Viceroy, Simla, 7 July 1909.
2. Government of India, Home Department, *Proceedings*, Political B, August 1909, Nos. 120-9.
3. *Ibid.*
4. The account on Shyamji Krishnavarma is based on Indulal Yajnik, *Shyamji Krishnavarma*; James Campbell Ker, *Political Troubles in India*; S.P. Sen, *Dictionary of National Biography*, Vol. IV, pp. 196-99; and *Proceedings* of the Home Department (Political), Government of India.
5. Emily C. Brown, *Har Dyal*, p. 22.
6. Ker, *op. cit.*, 170.
7. *Ibid.*
8. Brown, *op. cit*, p. 26.
9. *Ibid.*
10. Ker, *op. cit.*, p. 171. In 1896 the devastating plague epidemic broke out in Bombay which led to the enforcement of stringent measures by Rand, the Special Plague Commissioner, a haughty Englishman who became very unpopular in Poona. In 1897, Rand was associated at Poona by the Chapeker brothers who were hanged later.
11. Brown, *op. cit.*, p. 23.
12. *The Indian Sociologist*, July 1909, in *Trial Deposition of Madan Lal Dhingra* (National Archives of India).
13. David Garnet, *The Golden Echo*, p. 143.
14. Ker, *op. cit.*, p.174.
15. The account on Savarkar is based on his own writings besides Dhananjay Keer, *Veer Savarkar and His Times*; Ker, *op. cit.*, S.P. Sen, *op. cit.*, Vol. IV,

pp. 92-15; and the *Proceedings* of the Home Department. Keer's biography is eulogistic, and some statements are made without evidence; for example, see p. 52 wherein it is mentioned that Savarkar passed a pin through Dhingra's palm, and he remained unperturbed. Obviously this was to test Dhingra's courage, but Keer gives no evidence in support of his statement.

[16]Ker, *op. cit.*, p. 174.
[17]*Ibid.*, p. 176.
[18]*Ibid.*, p. 174.

[19]Sakharam Khare (1866-1928). Born on 1 August 1866 at Sangannar in the Ahmednager district; studied at Elphinstone College, Bombay; started legal practice in 1891 at Nasik; influenced by Tilak, Aurobindo, and Barinder Kumar Ghosh; was arrested in the Vande Matrem Case of 1906-07; implicated in Jackson Murder case in 1910; and was sentenced to four years imprisonment.

[20]Moderates' politics consisted in political advancement through constitutional means.

[21]Brown, *op. cit.*, p. 29.

[22]Ker, *op. cit*, pp. 174-75. Sirdarsinghji Rewabhai Rana born about 1878; a claimant to the chiefship of the State of Limbdi in Khathiawar; obtained B.A. from Bombay University, studied law at Gray's Inn at the same time earning his living by business; and was a close associate of Shyamji Krishnavarma and Savarkar.

[23]Sen, *op. cit.*, Vol. I, p. 135; Ker, *op. cit.*, pp. 397-99.

[24]Ker, *op. cit.*, pp. 198-99. Jawaharlal Nehru, *An Autobiography*, pp. 153-54.

[25]Keer, *op. cit.*, p. 28. See Government of India, Home Department, *Proceedings*, Political B, February 1919, No. 24, Letter from W. Colostream to Dunlop Smith, 8 January 1909.

[26]Vinayak Damodar Savarkar, *The Indian War of Independence*, 1857, Author's preface, p. XVI.

[27]*Ibid.*, p. 4.   [28]*Ibid.*, p. 199.   [29]*Ibid.*, pp. 7, 11.
[30]*Ibid.*, Authors' preface, p. ix.
[31]*Ibid.*, p. 20.   [32]*Ibid.*, p. 25.   [33]*Ibid.*, p. 66.
[34]*Ibid.*, pp. 67-68.   [35]*Ibid.*, p. 106.   [36]*Ibid.*, p. 108.
[37]*Ibid.*, p. 159.   [38]*Ibid.*, p. 205.   [39]*Ibid.*, p. 213.
[40]*Ibid.*, p. 218.   [41]*Ibid.*   [42]*Ibid.*, p. 261.
[43]*Ibid.*, p. 300.   [44]*Ibid.*, p. 391.

[45]*Ibid.*, p. 345. Cf. Carlyle, *Essays: Sir Walter Scott*, p. 280. How identical Savarkar's views are with those of Carlyle, particularly in ideas and rhetorical style which shows Carlyle's influence on Savarkar.

[46]Savarkar, *op. cit.*, p. 388.

[47]*Ibid.*, p. 373.   [48]*Ibid.*, p. 498.   [49]*Ibid.*, p. 498.

[50]*Ibid.*, p. 545. Noticing that the Badshai batteries were failing some one composed sarcastically the first verse, but the Emperor replied immediately that the sword of India would ply reaching England. See Mehdi Hussain, *Bahadur Shah II and the War of 1857 in Delhi with its Unforgettable Scenes*, pp. 45-46.

[51]Government of India, Home Department, *Proceedings*, Political B, June 1919, Nos. 105-24.

Notes

[52] Ker, *op. cit.*, pp. 172-73.
[53] *Ibid.*, p. 173.
[54] The second edition of Joseph Mazzini, *His Autobiography and Politics* (in Marathi), appeared in 1946, and was dedicated to Indian revolutionaries. Originally it was translated into Marathi in 1907.
[55] Savarkar, *Mazzini*, p. 5; Ker, *op. cit.*, pp. 185-86.
[56] Savarkar, *op. cit.*, pp. 20-21.
[57] *Ibid.*, pp. 19-21; Ker, *op. cit.*, pp. 185-86.
[58] See this Appeal in Appendix I, which was published on 10 July 1909, and reproduced from V.D. Savarkar, *The Indian War of Independence 1857*, pp. 546-94. James Campbell Ker, Senior Officer in the Home Department of the Indian Government, believed that this leaflet was the work of Shyamji Krishnavarma. See Ker, *op. cit.*, p. 176.
[59] Ker, *op. cit.*, p. 176; *The Times*, London, 23 May 1908, p. 10.
[60] Ker, *op. cit.*, pp. 107-08.
[61] *Ibid.*, p. 176.   [62] *Ibid.*, p. 177.
[63] Government of India, Home Department, *Proceedings*, Political B, February 1909, Nos. 2-11. According to Savarkar *Deg* meant principle of foundation, *Teg* sword and *Fateh*, victory. See Government of India, *Proceedings*, Political, Deposit, February 1909, No., 24. Cunningham defined *Deg* as Vassel for food, of grace. See J.D. Cunningham, *A History of the Sikhs*, p. 312.
[64] Appendix II. See also Government of India, Home Department, *Proceedings*, Political B, February 1909, Nos. 2-11. The song *Puggaree Sambhal O Jatta* is reproduced from S.C. Mittal. *Freedom Movement in Punjab*, p. 229; Government of India, Home Department, *Proceedings*, Political B, February, Nos. 133-15; Government of India, Home Department, *Proceedings*, February 1909, No. 24.
[65] (A) Ganesh Shrikrishan Khaparde (1854-1938). Born on 27 August 1854 at Inglol (Berar): passed LL.B. in 1884 from Bombay; started legal practice in 1890 at Amaroti, follower of Tilak; Chairman of the Reception Committee of the Amaroti Session of the Congress in 1897; was in England between August 1908 to November 1910 in connection with the appeal for Tilak's case in the Privy Council and later from May 1919 to January 1920 again in the UK to represent India's case on behalf of the Home Rule League and the Congress; and was elected to the Legislative Assembly during 1920-25.

(B) Lala Har Dyal (1884-1939). A great revolutionary and founder of Ghadr Party in the USA: born in 1884 in Delhi; was awarded a State scholarship for three years course of Postgraduate Studies at Oxford; came into contact with the revolutionaries like Shyamji Krishanvarma, V.D. Savarkar, etc.; started the *Bande Matram*, a monthly journal at Paris, left for the USA and started a paper *The Ghadr*; stayed in Sweden until 1927, and died in the USA on 4 March 1939.

(C) Ram Bhaj Dutt, Chaudhari (1866-1923). Born in a Mohyal family at Kanjrur Dattan, a village in Gurdaspur district; married Sarla Devi, who brought him into Freedom Struggle; participated in the Indian National Congress since 1888; took part in the Agrarian Movement in 1907 and the Anti-Rowlatt Agitation in April 1919; addressed a public meeting at Lahore on 11 April 1919; was arrested and deported to Dera Gahzi Khan, and released later. See Ker, op. cit., p. 177.

[66]Indulal Yajnik, *Shyamji Krishnavarma*, p. 266.

[67]Government of India, Home Department, *Proceedings*, Political B, July 1909, Nos. 66-73.

[68]Government of India, Home Department, *Proceedings*, Political B, November 1909, Nos. 32-46.

[69]Government of India, Home Department, *Proceedings*, Political B, July 1909, Nos. 66-73.

[70]*Ibid.*

[71]Ker, op. cit., p. 178. Mitra Mela was a secret organization formed by V.D. Savarkar in Nasik; in 1904 the name was changed to Abhinav Bharat with the object of extending its activities wider. When Savarkar left for England in 1906, his elder brother, Ganesh Vinayak Savarkar continued its activities until 1909 when he was arrested for publishing revolutionary literature, collecting weapons, and adopting seditious methods against the British Government. One of its members P.N. Bapat was sent to Paris for bomb-making. This organization had close contacts with other revolutionaries. See Ker, op. cit., p. 178.

[72]Ker, op. cit., p. 179.

[73]Garnet, op. cit., p. 143.

[74]*Ibid.*, p. 144.   [75]*Ibid.*, pp. 144-45.   [76]*Ibid.*, pp. 145-46.

[77]*Ibid.*, p. 76.   [78]*Ibid.*, p. 176.   [79]*Ibid.*, p. 78.

[80]Dhanajay Keer, *Veer Savarkar*, p. 36.

[81]Ker, op. cit., p. 178; Government of India, Home Department, *Proceedings*, Political B, May 1910, Nos. 133-35.

[82]Indulal Yajanik, op. cit., p. 262. Dharamvira, *Lala Hardyal and Revolutionary Movements of His Times*, p. 53.

[83]Government of India, Home Department, *Proceedings*, Political B, May 1910, Nos. 133-35. Yajnik, op. cit., p. 262.

[84]Bal Shastri Hardas, *Armed Struggle for Freedom*, p. 200. See also Sen, op. cit., p. 135.

[85]Government of India, Home Department, *Proceedings*, Political A, September 1909, Nos. 66-68. See also the Home Department, *Proceedings*, Political B, August 1909, Nos. 120-129, Ker, op. cit., 186.

[86]Government of India, Home Department, *Proceedings*, Political B, May 1910, Nos. 133-35.

[87]*Ibid.*

[88]David Garnet, op. cit., p. 147.

[89]Government of India, Home Department, *Proceedings*, Political B, May 1910, Nos. 133-35.

[90]*Ibid.*

[91]Government of India, Home Department, *Proceedings*, Political A, Nos. 66-68, p. 4.

CHAPTER 3

[1]*The Tribune*, 21 July 1909.

Notes

[2]This chapter is mainly based on the Trial Deposition of Madan Lal Dhingra which was recently acquired by the National Archives of India, New Delhi, from the Public Record Office, London.
[3]*The Statesman*, 4 July 1909.
[4]*The Times*, London, 3 July 1909; *Trial Deposition.*
[5]*Trial Deposition.*
[6]*Ibid.*, evidence of Madan Mohan Sinha.
[7]*Ibid.*, evidence of Douglas William Thorburn.
[8]*Ibid.*, evidence of Sir Leslie Probyn.
[9]*Ibid.*, evidence of Madan Mohan Sinha.
[10]*Ibid.*, evidence of Sir Leslie Probyn.
[11]*Ibid.*
[12]*Ibid.*, evidence of Charles Rollestone.
[13]*Ibid.*, evidence of Charles Rollestone and Fredrick Nicholas.
[14]Quoted from *The Indian Sociologist*, 21 July 1909 in *Trial Deposition.*
[15]*The Tribune*, 21 July 1909.
[16]*Trial Deposition*, evidence of Albert Draper.
[17]*Ibid.*
[18]*The Tribune*, 2 July 1909.
[19]Government of India, Home Department, *Proceedings*, Political B, May 1910, Nos. 133-35; see also the same series, B, September 1909, Nos. 47-54.
[20]Government of India, Home Department, *Proceedings*, Political B, September 1909, Nos. 47-54.
[21]*Office Diary of Khaparade Papers*, 22 July 1909, p. 203.
[22]*Trial Deposition*, evidence of Charles Glass.
[23]*Ibid.*, evidence of Ilbert Issac.
[24]W.S. Blunt, *My Diaries*, Vol. II, pp. 269-70.
[25]*The Tribune*, 25 July 1909.
[26]*Ibid.*, 13 August 1909, see also Blunt, *op. cit.*, pp. 269-70.
[27]*Trial Deposition*, statement by Dhingra.
[28]David Garnet, *The Golden Echo*, p. 148.
[29]Blunt, *op. cit.*, pp. 461-62.
[30]M.N. Das, *India Under Morley and Minto*, p. 142.
[31]Government of India Home Department, *Proceedings*, Political B, October 1909, Nos. 110-17.
[32]Blunt, *op. cit.*, pp. 461-62.
[33]*Ibid.*
[34]Khaparde Diary, *op. cit.*, 31 July 1919, p. 212.
[35]Government of India, Home Department, *Proceedings*, Political B, August 1909, No. 64.
[36]*The Civil and Military Gazette*, 19 August 1909.
[37]Government of India, Home Department, *Proceedings*, Political B, August 1909, No. 64.

Madan Lal Dhingra's remains were brought to India at Palam Airport on 13 December 1976; and Mukand Lal Dhingra, Madan's nephew, tells their story in his letter to this writer dated 27 June 1977.

I feel that our Government came to know about it (Madan Lal had been buried after his execution) at the time of taking the remains of Udham

Singh (who had shot O'Dwyer and was hanged for it). My eldest brother Dr Hira Lal Dhingra known as Dr H. Lal of New Delhi wrote to me last year that he had met a British journalist in Delhi who disclosed to him that all the persons who were executed in Pentonville Jail were buried there in the cemetry. Punjab Government asked me to pay the exhumation charges of the remains of Madan Lal from Pentonville Jail. In reply I informed that I was not gainfully employed after retirement in 1973 and it was very difficult for me to make even both ends meet. The British Home Secretary also refused to give their consent for the exhumation of the remains, and in case three (3) persons next to him request for this, it can be considered. Accordingly myself and my two sons applied for this through Punjab Government. The exhumation took place in the presence of K. Natwar Singh, then acting as Indian High Commissioner in London, who brought the remains after exhumation to India.

[38] Blunt, *op. cit.*, pp. 461-62.

CHAPTER 4

[1] Government of India, Home Department, *Proceedings*, Political B, August 1909, Nos. 120-29; Dr Rajan's account.
[2] Stanley A. Wolpert, *Morley and India*, p. 124.
[3] *Ibid.*
[4] *Trial Deposition*, Letter from Lt. Col. W.H.C. Wyllie to Madan Lal Dhingra, 13 April 1909.
[5] Government of India, Home Department, *Proceedings*, Political A, September 1909, Nos. 66-68. See also *Trial Deposition*: E.J. Beck to Madan Lal, 5 May 1909.
[6] Government of India, Home Department, *Proceedings*, Political A, September 1909, Nos. 66-68. This file contains letter from the members of the Dhingra family to the British authorities and some of these have been reproduced by Martin Gilbert in *Servant of India*, pp. 192-96.
[7] *Lascar:* It is rather difficult to set facts right for want of evidence. Why did Dhingra join as *lascar*, it is not possible to say with any certainty. One might only conjecture but from the family correspondence it seems that after six months service as a *lascar*, he returned to Amritsar, and it was later that he went to England. Therefore, the view that he ran away from home and joined as a *lascar* and proceeded to England on his own without any support from his family does not seem to be correct.
[8] Government of India, Home Department, *Proceedings*, Political A, September 1909, Nos., 66-68, Letter from Dunlop Smith to the Viceroy.
[9] Government of India, Home Department, *Proceedings*, Political A, September 1909 from Amritsar, 5 July 1909.
[10] *Trial Deposition*, Report from S.R. Dyer, H.M. Prison, 2 July 1909.
[11] Blunt, *My Diaries*, Vol. II, pp. 262-63.
[12] Government of India, Home Department, *Proceedings*, Political A, September 1909, Nos. 66-8; Secretary of State for India to Viceroy (Pro. No. 68), 14 August 1909.

Notes

13 *Trial Deposition*, evidence by Mary Harris.
14 *Ibid.*, evidence of E.J. Beck.
15 *Trial Deposition.*
16 Savarkar, *Six Glorious Epochs of Indian History*, p. 418.
17 *Ibid.*, p. 469.
18 *Trial Deposition*, evidence from Alfred Draper.
19 *Ibid.*, evidence from Henry Stanton Morley.
20 *Ibid.*
21 *Ibid.*, evidence from Mary Harris. Bhang is a narcotic drug obtained from the Indian hemp.
22 Government of India, Home Department, *Proceedings*, Political A, September 1909, Nos. 66-68. See also letter from Dr Mohan Lal Dhingra and Dr Behari Lal Dhingra to the Private Secretary to the Viceroy, 7 July 1909.
23 *Trial Deposition.*
24 *Ibid.*, evidence of Charles Rollestone.
25 Government of India, Home Department, *Proceedings*, Political B, September 1909, Nos. 47-56.
26 *Trial Deposition*, evidence of Emma Joseph Beck.
27 *Ibid.*
28 Government of India, Home Department, *Proceedings*, Political B, September 1909, Nos. 47-54.
29 Government of India, Home Department, *Proceedings*, Political B, August 1909, Nos., 120-29.
30 *Ibid.*
31 *Ibid.*, *Guru* means preceptor and *Avatar*, incarnation.
32 *Ibid.* 33 *Ibid.* 34 *Ibid.* 35 *Ibid.*
36 *Ibid.*
37 Appendix III.

CHAPTER 5

1 Stanely A. Wolpert, *Morley and India*, p. 124.
2 *Ibid*
3 Government of India, Home Department, *Proceedings*, Political A, September 1909, Nos. 66-68.
4 *Ibid.* 5 *Ibid.* 6 *Ibid.*
7 *Ibid.*, see Letter from Dr Mohan Lal and Dr Behari Lal to the Private Secretary to the Viceroy, Simla, 7 July 1909; Government of India, Home Department, *Proceedings*, Political A, September 1909, Nos. 66-68.
8 *Ibid.* 9 *Ibid.* 10 *Ibid.* 11 *Ibid.*
12 *Ibid.* 13 *Ibid.* 14 *Ibid.* 15 *Ibid.*
16 *Ibid.* 17 *Ibid.*
18 *The Tribune*, 13 July 1909.
19 Government of India, Home Department, *Proceedings*, Political A, September 1909, Nos. 66-8.
20 *Khaparade Diary*, 2 July 1909, p. 184.

[21] V.N. Datta and Cleghorn, *A Muslim Nationalist and Indian Politics*, pp. 118-89.
[22] Khaparde, *op. cit.*, p. 186.
[23] B.S. Maighowalia, *Indian Martyr Executed in Pentonvellie, London on 17 August 1909*, p. 27.
[24] Government of India, Home Department, *Proceedings*, Political B, August 1909, Nos. 120-29; see Ker, *op. cit.*, p. 54.
[25] Khaparde, *op. cit.*, 5 July 1909, p. 186.
[26] Quoted from *The Times*, London, 6 July 1909, in Government of India, Home Department, *Proceedings*, Political B, August 1909, Nos. 120-29.
[27] *The Civil and Military Gazette*, 11 July 1909.
[28] *Debates of the Legislative Council of Bengal*, 13 July 1909.
[29] *Gokhale Papers*: File Nos. 203-13, Part III.
[30] *Ibid.*
[31] Mohandas K. Gandhi, *The Collected Works of Mahatma Gandhi*, Vol. IX (1908-09), p. 302.
[32] *Ibid.*
[33] *Ibid.*, pp. 302-03; Gandhi criticized Dhingra's statement in which he had said that if the Germans attacked Englishmen then the English had the right to attack any one of the Germans, even though he might be pacifist To Gandhi this was a fallacy.
[34] *Ibid.*, Vol. X, p. 4.   [35] *Ibid.*
[36] *Ibid.*, p. 42.
[37] *The Tribune*, 7 July 1909.
[38] *Parliamentary Debates* (Official Report), House of Commons, Eighth Volume of Series, July 1909 to 6 August 1909 (col. 1360-61).
[39] *The Tribune*, 7 July 1909.
[40] *The Tribune*, 6 August 1909.
[41] *The Tribune*, 9 July 1909.
[42] *Parliamentary Debates*, *op. cit.*, col. 842.
[43] Gilbert, *Martin, Servant of India*, p. 195.
[44] *Ibid.*
[45] *Ibid.* Loharu was a semi-independent state under the control of the Commissioner of Delhi. The Newab was King Lord in 1897, and from 1899 to 1901 was a member of the Legislative Council of Punjab; see also countless of Mary Minto, *India: Minto and Morley, 1905-1911*, p. 315.
[46] *The Parliamentary Debates* (Official Reports), House of Commons, Tenth Volume of Session, from 30 August to September 1909, col. 18.
[47] Indulal Yajnik, *Life and Times of an Indian Revolutionary*, p. 27.
[48] *Ibid.*
[49] Gilbert, *op. cit.*, pp. 194-95.
[50] Emily C. Brown, *Har Dyal*, p. 75.
[51] *Ibid.*
[52] Blunt, *op. cit.*, pp. 269-70.
[53] *Ibid*, p. 262.
[54] *Ibid.*, p. 276.
[55] Gilbert, *op. cit.*, p. 194.
[56] M.N. Das, *India Under Morley and Minto*, p. 142.

Notes

[57] *Ibid.*, p. 144.
[58] Viscount John Morley, *Recollections*, Vol. 2, p. 313.
[59] Ker, *op. cit.*, p. 181.
[60] Wolpert, *op. cit.*, p. 124.
[61] *Ibid.*, p. 125.
[62] *Ibid.*
[63] Blunt, *op. cit*, pp. 269-70.

CHAPTER 6

[1] See Appendix IV.
[2] Usually impotence is psychological, and whatever the primary cause, the disorders as a result of anxiety and shame tend to become self-perpetuating. See *A Short Guide to Mental Illness*, p. 94.
[3] *Ibid.*, p. 26.

Bibliography

UNPUBLISHED SOURCES*

Proceedings of the Home Department (Political), Government of India (Confidential), 1900-1912.

PRIVATE PAPERS.

The Dhingra Family Papers (available with G.R. Sethi, Rai Bahadur Rattan Chand Road, and with Mukand Lal Dhingra, 8 Dasaundha Singh Road, at Amritsar).
Gopal Krishna Gokhale Papers.
G.S. Khaparade Papers.
G.S. Khaparde Diary.
Lord Morley Papers (Microfilm available at Nehru Memorial Museum and Library, New Delhi).
Lord Minto Papers.
Trial Deposition of Madan Lal Dhingra.
Letters from Mukand Lal Dhingra and Mrs Shukla Hari Dass (with this writer).

PUBLISHED DOCUMENTS

Legislative Council Debates of Bengal 1909.
Parliamentary Debates (official reports) (House of Commons, 1908-1910).

PERIODICALS AND NEWSPAPERS.

The Civil and Military Gazette, Lahore, 1909, Microfilm available at Nehru Memorial Museum and Library, New Delhi.
Jan Pradeep, Hindi, Jullundur, 1968.
The Statesman, Calcutta, 1909-1910.
The Times, London, 1908-1909.
The Tribune, Lahore, 1907-1910, 1970.

OTHER WORKS

A Short Guide to Mental Illness, May and Baker Limited, 1907.
Blunt, W.S., *My Diaries (1900-1914)*, Vol. II, London, 1919.

---

*All these documents are available at the National Archives of India, New Delhi, unless otherwise mentioned.

Brown, Emily, C., *Har Dayal*, New Delhi, 1975.
Cunningham, J.D., *A History of the Sikhs*, New Delhi, 1972.
Das, M.N., *India Under Morley and Minto*, London, 1964.
Datta, Braham Nath, *The Martyrdom of Madan Lal Dhingra*, Ludhiana, 1976.
―――, *Amar Saheed Madan Lal Dhingra*, 1975.
Datta, V.N., *Jallianwala Bagh*, Ludhiana, 1967.
―――, *Amirtsar: Past and Present*, Amritsar, 1967.
Datta, V.N. and B. Cleghorn, *A Muslim Nationalist and Indian Politics*, Delhi, 1974.
Deshpande, A.K., *Hutatama Madan Lal Dhingra*, Poona.
Dharmvira, *Lala Har Dyal and Revolutionary Movement of His Times*, New Delhi, 1970.
Gandhi, M.K., *The Collected Works of Mahatma Gandhi*, Vols. VIII and IX, Ahmedabad, 1963.
Garnet, David, *The Golden Echo*, New York, 1954.
Gilbert, Martin, *The Servant of India, A Story of Imperial Rule from 1905-1910 as told through the Correspondence and Diaries of James Dunlop Smith, P.A. to Viceroy*, London, 1966.
Hardas, Bal Shastri, *Armed Struggle for Ninety Years 1857-1947*, Poona, 1958.
Harrison, Fredric (ed.), "Caryle" in *Essays*, Blackie, London.
Hussain, Mehadi, *Bahadur Shah II and the War of 1857 in Delhi with its Unforgettable Scenes*, Delhi, 1958.
Keer, Dhananjay, *Veer Savarkar and His Times*, Bombay, 1950.
Ker, James Campbell, *Political Trouble in India, 1907-1917*, Delhi, Ferozepur, 1917, reprinted in 1973.
Maighowalia, B.S., *First Indian Martyr Executed in Pentonveille*, Hoshiarpur, 1975.
Mary Minto, Countess, *India, Minto and Morley*, London, 1908.
Mittal, S.C., *Freedom Movement in Punjab (1905-1929)*, New Delhi, 1977.
Morley, John Viscount, *Recollections*, Vol. II, London, 1918.
Nehru, Jawaharlal, *An Autobiography*, London, 1958.
Pearay Mohan, *An Imaginary Rebellion: How it was Suppressed*, Lahore, 1920.
Savarkar, V.D., *The Indian War of Independence 1857*, New Delhi, 1970.
―――, *Mazzini* (2nd edn), Poona, 1946.
―――, *Six Glorious Epochs of Indian History*, Bombay, 1971.
Sen, S.P., *Dictionary of National Biography*, Vols. I to IV, Calcutta, 1972-74.
Walpert, Stanley A., *Morley and India (1906-1910)*, California, 1967.
Yajnik, Indulal, *Shyamji Krishnavarma: Life and Times of an Indian Revolutionary*, Bombay, 1950.

Index

Abhinav Bharat, 12-14; branches of, 30
Aga Khan, and Wyllie's murder, 67, 68
Aiyer, V.V.S., 13-15, 20, 38, 80; tribute to Dhingra's act, 57
All India Congress Committee, and Dhingra's act, 73
Ameer Ali, Syed, Wyllie's murder condemned by, 68, 73, 74
Amin, Govind, 13, 30
Amritsar, 3-5; political activities in, 3; Sir Michael O'Dwyer's views on, 3, 4
Arora, Harnam Singh, 13
Arya Samaj, ideology and programme of, 9
Azim-ullah, 91

Bahadur Shah, 90
Baji Rao, 17
Baker, Sir Edward, and Wyllie's murder, 70
Baksh, Sheikh Umar, Dhingra's act condemned by, 73
Balkrishna, heroic example of, 12
Bande Matram, 28, 41
Banerjee, Surendra Nath, 67
Bapat, Gandurang Mahadev, 13-15, 31, 80; and bomb-making formula, 30; education and family background of, 14
Beck, Emma Josephine, evidence of, 47, 50, 54, 55
Bhandari, Sir Todur Mul, 4, 5
Bhatt, Gaga, 17
Bhownaggree, Sir M., and Wyllie's murder, 68

Blunt, W.S., praise for Dhingra's act, 77
Bomb-making philosophy, 30, 85
Bose, Khudi Ram, execution of, 15, 27
Bose, Rash Behari, and Ghadr agitation, 3
British repressive methods, condemnation by Savarkar, 26, 27
British rule, admiration for, 5; criticism of, 10; methods suggested for fighting against, 24, 25; Savarkar's hatred for, 12
Buchanan, and Wyllie's murder, 54, 55

Carnac, J.D., evidence of, 50
Carmichael, D.E., 32
Cawnpore massacre, 19, 20
Chapekar brothers, heroic example of, 11
Chatterjee, Sarojini, 4, 14
Chattopadhyaya, Birendra Nath, 13, 80; family background of, 14
Chatturbhajn, 80
Churchill, Winston, 77
Clarke, Sir Synenham, and Wyllie's murder, 59
Curzon, Lord, criticism of, 10; Dhingra and, 57, 81, 82; repressive policy of, 15, 45

Dalhousie, Lord, policy of comprehensive annexations, 17
Damodar, Ganesh, role in politics, 12
Dane, Sir Louis, 65, 66
Das, Dwarkar, 42

Das, Mrs Shukla Hari, on Dhingra's marriage, 95
Dass, Hem Chandra, 30
Das, Nitisen, 31
Daulat Ram, Rai Bahadur, 2
Dayanand, Swami, meeting with Krishnavarma, 9
Dhingra, Behari Lal, on Dhingra's act, 61, 62; on British Government, 6
Dhingra, Bhajan Lal, 31, 49; meeting with Dhingra in prison, 38
Dhingra, Chaman Lal, 1,2,5,6, 64
Dhingra, H.L., on Dhingra's marriage, 95
Dhingra, Kundan Lal, and Wyllie's murder, 60,61; correspondence with Wyllie 46, 47
Dhingra, Madan Lal, and Wyllie, 46, 81, 82; arrest of, 37, 38; assassination of Wyllie by, 8, 32, 33; association with British officials, 1; association with India House activities, 30, 31; association with Savarkar, 13, 81; birth of, 1; childhood of, 83; charges against, 38, 39; criticism of his act, 66-80; education of, 1; erratic behaviour of, 81; examples of courage, 85; examples of curious behaviour of, 48, 49; execution of, 41-43, 66, 80; family background of, 1; father's attitude towards, 2; Indian public opinion about, 84, 85; marriage, 95; moments of psychological crisis, 83, 84; motive for Wyllie's murder, 44-58, personality of, 3; statement in the court, 39-41; trial of, 41
Dhingra, Mohan Lal, education of, 1; and Wyllie's murder, 63, 65
Dhingra, Mukand Lal, on Dhingra's marriage, 95
Dhingra, Sahib Ditta Mal, assets of, 1; contribution of, 96; death of, 95; fascination for England, 2; impact of Wyllie's murder on, 62, 63; personality of, 1, 2; position of, 5; relations with Dunlop Smith, 5
Dhingra family, and Wyllie episode, 49, 50, 61-66; educational background of, 2; migration of, 1; relations with British officials, 2, 5, 6; relations with Wyllie, 46, 81, 82; status of, 2
Draper, Albert, 52; and Wyllie's murder, 37
Duff, Sir Mounstuart Grant, 32
Dutt, Ram Bhaj, 26
Dutta, S.K., on Dhingra's motive for Wyllie's murder, 45

Ebrahim, Fazulboy Currimboy, 33
Elgin, Lord, 9
English people, temperament of, 7
English Press, and Wyllie's assassination, 77
Extremists, Krishnavarma's admiration for, 10

Free Indian Society, establishment of, 13

Gagar Mal, position of, 5
Gandhi, M.K., and Wyllie's murder condemned by, 71-73
Garibaldi, 12
Garnet, David, 10; meeting with Dhingra, 31; on Dhingra's statement in the court, 40, 41; report on Savarkar and India House, 27, 28
George, Llyod, praise for Dhingra's act, 77
Ghadr agitation, 3
Glass, Charles, 38, 39
Gokhale, 52; Wyllie's murder condemned by, 69, 70, 79
Grayson, Victor, on Wyllie's murder, 77, 78

Har Dayal, tribute to Dhingra's act, **76-77**

Index

Hardie, Keir, and Wyllie's murder, 74
Harkishan Lal, Wyllie's murder condemned by, 73
Harris, Mary, evidence of, 50-54
Harrison, Frank, impact of, 9
Hirtzel, Fredrik Arthur, on Wyllie's murder, 45, 79
Hudelston, 32
Hyndman, H.M., study of India's political problems by, 9

Institute of Imperial Studies, London, 32, 33
India House, founding of, 10; Krishnavarma's control over, 13; Dhingra's visit to, 7; revolutionary activities in, 8, 14, 15, 25, 26, 27
India House revolutionaries, praise for Dhingra's act, 84
Indian Home Rule Society (1905), founding of, 9
Indian Mutiny, lessons of, 90
Indian political elite, and Dhingra's act, 73-75
Indian public opinion, and Wyllie's murder, 79
Indian revolutionaries, role of, 8
Indians, British attitude towards, 7
Intelligence reports of Scotland Yard, and Dhingra's motive for Wyllie's murder, 45

Jackson, murder of, 79

Kaki Rani, 2
Ken, James Campbell, on Wyllie's murder, 78, 79
Khan, Ali, 30
Khan Bahadur, 4
Khan, Malik Umar Hayat, and Dhingra's act, 73
Khan, Sir Amir-ud-Din Ahmad, Wyllie's murder condemned by, 74, 75
Khaparade, G.S., 26, 38, 42; condemnation of Wyllie's murder by, 67, 79
Khare, Sakharan, 12
King Edward VII, and Wyllie's murder, 74, 75
Koregaonkar, H.K., 31, 38, 80; evidence of, 55-57
Krishnavarma, Shyamji, and Savarkar, 12, 13; architect of the revolutionary movement in England, 8; as a lawyer, 8; contribution of, 10, 11; Dewan in Ratlam and Junagarh, 8; education of, 8; meeting with Swami Dayanand, 9; member of the State Council, Udaipur, 8; praise for Madan's act, 70, 71, 75; programme of, 15; relation with Wyllie, 46

Lakshmi Bai, heroic example of, 17
Lal, Babu Kanhaya, 4
Lalcaca, Cawas, assassination of, 32, 38, 43, 65, 68, 71
Lyall, Lady, evidence of, 56
Lyall, Sir Charles, 33, evidence of, 56

Maclagan, Sir Edward, on Amritsar, 4
Maharaja Pratap Singh of Jammu and Kashmir, 1
Maharana Pratap, heroic example of, 12
Majithia, Sunder Singh, 4
Malaviya, Pandit Madan Mohan, Dhingra's act condemned by, 73
Master, S.M., application for the prevention of Dhingra's execution, 41, 42
Mehra, Rattan Chand, 4
Minto, Lord, 5, 60, 74, 75
Miranjan, 21
Morley, John S., 30
Morley, Henry Stanton, account of Dhingra's shooting practice, 52-54

Index

Morley, Lady, and Wyllie's murder, 59
Morley, Lord, 32, 43, 45, 81, 82
Morrison, Theodore, and Wyllie's murder, 67, 68
Muzzaffurpur Bomb Case (1908), 5, 64

Naidu, 31
Nana Sahib, 17, 19, 26
Nand Lal, 4
Nasik Conspiracy Case, 80
National Indian Association, aims of, 33
Narang, Gokal Chand, on Guru Gobind Singh, 26
Nawab of Loharu, Wyllie's murder condemned by, 74, 75
Nehru, Jawaharlal, 93
Nicholas, Fredrick, and Wyllie's murder, 37

O'Dwyer, Sir Michael, on Amritsar, 3, 4
Oriental Conference in Berlin (1881), Krishnavarma's representation in, 8

Pal, B.C., 11, 52; condemnation of Wyllie's murder by, 67, release of, 25
Pandey, Mangal, 18, 19
Parikh, J.M., 22; condemnation of Wyllie's murder by, 67
Phadke, W.V., 14
Pandit, Kotu Mal, 4
Paranjpe, S.M., 22
Partition of Bengal, 15; Savarkar on, 11, 12
Partition of India, 93
Phyare, General, 32
Pingley, Vishnu Ganesh, and making of bomb, 3
Probyn, Sir Leslie, account of Wyllie's murder, 34, 35

Rajan, T.S., 38
Rana, S.R., 13, 80

Revolver-training centre, London, 30
Rolleston, Charles, interrogation with Dhingra, 36; and Wyllie's murder, 54, 55
Revolt of 1857, 50th anniversary of, 15, 23, 24, 89-92
Revolutionary activities in Paris, 13, 79-81
Revolutionary movement, 8, 10; programme of, 51
Russia, Japan's victory over and Krishnavarma's admiration for, 10
Russian intelligentia, 82

Sadiq, Khawaja Ghulam, 5
Sandeman, Sir Robert, 32
Sanyal, Sachin, and *Ghadr* agitation, 3
Savarkar, Ganesh, imprisonment of, 27
Savarkar, Vinayak Damodar, 10, 31, 40, 46; and Krishnavarma, 12, 13; and Dhingra, 13, 51, 52, 81, and Tilak, 12; arrest of, 79, 80; birth of, 11; bomb-making philosophy of, 85; education of 11; personality of, 12; speech on the 50th anniversary of the mutiny of 1857, 89-92; Shivaji scholarship to, 11; programme of, 15
Sen, Keshub Chunder, 2
Sethi, G.R., 1
Shah, Bahadur, 20, 21
Shah, Pir Ali, 91
Shivaji, heroic example of, 17; inspiration from, 12
Sikh community, 8, 26
Singh, Ajit, 15
Singh, Guru Gobind, birth centenary of, 25, 26
Singh, Harnam, 14, 26, 38, 40
Sinha, Madan Mohan, 36
Singh, Maharaja Ranjit, 4
Singh, Sardar Jeewan, 5
Smith, Dunlop, 5, 6, 48, 62-64

Index

Spencer, Herbert, 9, 12
Stevenson-Moore, C.J., 31
Stevens, Lyne, and Wyllie's murder, 77
Sukh, Pandit Sarb, 4
Swaraj, principles of, 16, 18
Swadeshi movement, 12, 15
Syed Mamud, 93

Thorburn, Douglas William, and Wyllie's murder, 34
Tilak, B.G., 22; and Savarkar, 11, 12; arrest of, 15, 27; inspiration from, 12; Krishnavarma's admiration for, 10
Tirumalacharya, M.P., 68

Varma, Gyan Chand, 14, 31
Violence, Krishnavarma's belief in, 10; Savarkar's belief in, 18

War of Independence of 1857, anniversary of, 15, 22
William, Sir Monier, 8
Wyllie, Lady Curzon, 36
Wyllie, Sir William Curzon, 32, 44, 46, 47, 67-70; assassination of, 8, 32-43; correspondence with Kundan Lal, 46, 47; impact of his assassination in India and England, 59-62; motive for murder of, 44-58